"In this memorable collection, Erin Hicks Moon narrates her personal journey through the landscape of American cultural Christianity, one with which an entire generation of Christians will relate. With the mind of a teacher, the heart of a friend, and a charming sense of humor, Erin provides a generous and important contribution to the deconstruction conversation, offering a thoughtful and nuanced critique of her faith expression without dishonoring her faith. Her stories resonate and her writing sings."

Emily P. Freeman, *New York Times* bestselling author of
How to Walk into a Room

"Erin Hicks Moon is a refreshingly honest companion for those no longer satisfied with a laundry list of spiritual certainties. Reflecting on a lifetime spent asking questions (and sometimes avoiding them), Moon invites readers to consider the 'little plots of land' on which we encounter God—to set fire to the weeds that choke them and allow something wild and new to emerge from their ashes. Settle in for a conversation with the best friend you've never met—a trustworthy guide on any faith journey (drink!)."

Pete Enns, host of *The Bible for Normal People* podcast
and author of *Curveball: When Your Faith
Takes Turns You Never Saw Coming*

"For many Christians, heartache, exhaustion, and rage have become debilitatingly commonplace. Is this whole faith thing even worth it anymore? Erin Moon doesn't offer an answer but contextualizes the beauty of asking the question. Full of empathy, wisdom, and a mountain of zingers, *I've Got Questions* is a hall pass for the spiritually weary."

Kendra Adachi, *New York Times* bestselling author of
The Lazy Genius Way

"Not since *Searching for Sunday* by Rachel Held Evans have I come across a book that so vividly describes the grief, pain, and beauty of deconstructing and reconstructing faith. I couldn't make it through the introduction without both tearing up and audibly laughing. Erin Moon's *I've Got Questions: The Spiritual Practice of Having It Out with God* was a balm for my soul and I anticipate that it will be my most given away book of the year."

Zach W. Lambert, lead pastor of Restore
and co-founder of the Post Evangelical Collective

"*I've Got Questions* is for anyone who has felt like maybe what they wonder is not allowed, like maybe they're the only one not settled on this or that point yet. But more than permission to ask, Erin is inviting us to practice this truth: any faith worth having, any God worth trusting, is one where everything is askable. Erin is skilled at naming the things that swirl in our hearts and minds, and by naming them, they sift and sort. Then we find ourselves feeling not just clearer, but less alone, like we have a companion in our questions. This book is a gift for all of us to help us carry questions well."

Meredith Miller, pastor and author of *Woven:
Nurturing a Faith Your Kid Doesn't Have to Heal From*

I'VE GOT
QUESTIONS

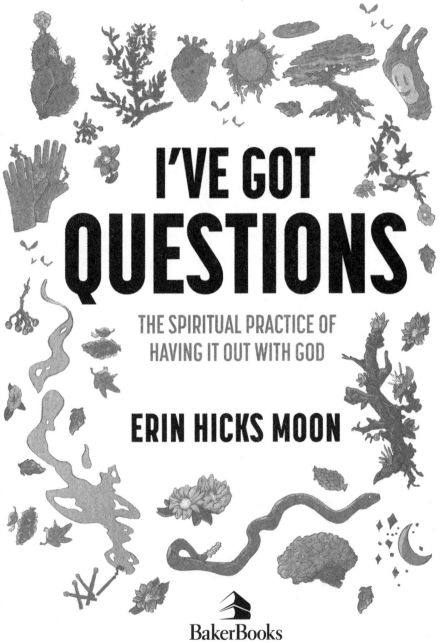

I'VE GOT
QUESTIONS

THE SPIRITUAL PRACTICE OF
HAVING IT OUT WITH GOD

ERIN HICKS MOON

BakerBooks

a division of Baker Publishing Group
Grand Rapids, Michigan

Published by Baker Books
a division of Baker Publishing Group
Grand Rapids, Michigan
BakerBooks.com

Printed in the United States of America

Library of Congress Cataloging-in-Publication Data
Names: Moon, Erin Hicks, 1983– author. Title: I've got questions : the spiritual practice of having it out with God / Erin Hicks Moon.
Description: Grand Rapids, Michigan : Baker Books, a division of Baker Publishing Group, [2025] | Includes bibliographical references.
Identifiers: LCCN 2024023181 | ISBN 9781540904089 (cloth) | ISBN 9781493449187 (ebook)
Subjects: LCSH: Baptists—Texas. | Christian life. | Spirituality.
Classification: LCC BX6248.T4 M66 2025
LC record available at https://lccn.loc.gov/2024023181

Cover illustration by Nate Eidenberger

Some names and details have been changed to protect the privacy of the individuals involved.

The author is represented by The Christopher Ferebee Agency, www.christopherferebee.com.

Baker Publishing Group publications use paper produced from sustainable forestry practices and postconsumer waste whenever possible.

25 26 27 28 29 30 31   7 6 5 4 3 2 1

To my parents,
who offered a gospel so rich and real,
it made all the false versions easier to kill.

CONTENTS

FOREWORD

One of the greatest gifts we offer to one another is the reminder we aren't alone. And that is no small thing for those
of us who found ourselves at the threshold of the wilderness,
deconstructing everything we thought we knew about God,
the universe, the Bible, our communities, our churches, and
even ourselves. It can be a snarly, sad, complicated, costly,
and even scary experience.

We all have our own story of how we landed here. Yours
will be unique to you. But throughout all my years alongside
folks disentangling their faith, there are two things I've found
to be pretty consistent for many of us: this is a profoundly
unshepherded stage of faith formation and it is deeply lonely.
I wish that wasn't true. But it usually is. So we go looking
for guides and companions.

Enter all the so-called "experts" showing up on social
media and in church spaces to warn about the dangers and
the ills of deconstruction, to layer shame and guilt on top
of your disorientation and fear, to mock or belittle your
very real questions and doubts. Now, in addition to feeling

unmoored from everything that you used to know as truth, you wonder if you're broken or bad or even sinful.

Or perhaps you find yourself in circles that wish you would just throw out all of it—the bathwater and the baby—when it comes to your faith, telling you that everything about Christianity is wrong and bad and unredeemable. (To be honest, there are days when I understand why people land there.)

I do not believe that God is clutching their pearls over your honest seeking of truth, nor do I think you need to renounce everything you once loved or hoped about God. As my own father told me at a very key crossroad in my own journey, I'm not afraid for you. If you're honestly seeking God, you will find God, even if it looks very different than what I've found. So even if folks in your life are convinced that you should "just have faith like a child" (one of my least favorite misuses of Scripture because anyone who uses that phrase as shorthand for squashing questions has clearly never spent time with a kid), or if you are being accused of faithlessness, or even if you're genuinely asking why you bother, you're in the right place.

I believe with my whole heart that you've landed here at the invitation of the Spirit. So this isn't time to panic nor is it time to pretend to be fine or to rush to new certainties. No, this is the time to fully live into the season of wrestling and questioning and discerning to which the Spirit has called you. Far from a sign of apostasy, I believe your own wilderness season of faith will actually become an altar of intimacy with God and genuine transformation for you. You're in exactly the right place at the right time. You're also deeply held in the love and the welcome and the goodness of God, no matter what you think (or don't think) about penal substitutionary atonement or church attendance or voter guides now.

But that good work doesn't happen alone. You were right, you do need companions and guides, just as you have needed them in every other stage of your development. And this is the part of the foreword where I take you by the hand and lead you over to my friend Erin Hicks Moon and tell you that this is someone you can trust wholeheartedly for this leg of the journey. You're in good hands in these pages.

To say that Erin Moon is deeply beloved is as vast an understatement as I can imagine. People *love* Erin. They love her witty and weird podcast, her internet presence, her newsletter, her books. They love her authenticity, humor, wisdom, curiosity, and resolute kindness. They love her stories, whether sad or hilarious. They adore her quirks and her foibles, her ability to translate complicated theological ideas into actually helpful guidance, her theater-kid energy, her questionable taste in movies, and her Texas-sized ability to call bullshit.

Of course, I say that "people love Erin," but we all know that I also mean "Sarah Bessey loves Erin Hicks Moon" for those very things. But I also love her for her deep faithfulness, her thoughtful compassion, her inclusive gospel-centered goodness, her truth-telling about how we got here, her refusal to be anyone's hero or guru, and her inimitable voice. I mean, what other spiritual leader do you know who will drop Baby-Sitters Club and Taco Bell Crunchwrap Supreme references alongside beautiful thoughts on resurrection and justice that make you want to rededicate your life to Jesus?

As you wrestle with your spiritual inheritance, discerning what to discard and what to hold as precious, Erin does that important work of reminding you that you aren't alone. You are part of a faithful historic community of believers who have been invited to wrestle with God and be changed. As she reminds us, "Having it out with God is your spiritual heritage. The wrestling is not the problem, it is the point." You're part of a vast company of folks out here who are learning—sometimes the hard way—that God is more welcoming, more loving, more inclusive, and more generous than we ever imagined. And that love gives you room: room for your questions, room for your story, room for your hopes, room for your grief and your anger, room for your transformation, and room for your whole self. One of the things I've loved about Erin's work is that she doesn't stop at your own self, either: she then turns us around to encounter this beautiful, broken world that God so loves. She reminds us that our healing isn't just for ourselves, it's for the sake of the world too.

As someone who first experienced that disorientation and loneliness of an evolving faith more than twenty years ago, I confess I'm a bit jealous that you have someone like Erin at your side for this journey. There is a hospitality to Erin's work that makes room for the full truth—not just the hard and painful truths but the beautiful and strong truths too. She's the funny, smart, bitingly honest, turn-over-tables-in-the-temple instigator you needed to name the things you can't say out loud. And she is the steadfastly hopeful, stubbornly faithful, tenderhearted, generous, and trustworthy guide who will lead you back to what you always hoped was true all along.

Alongside you,

Sarah Bessey
bestselling author of *Field Notes for the Wilderness*
and *A Rhythm of Prayer*

INTRODUCTION

Divination in the Southern Baptist Church

You don't often get fortune-telling in a Baptist church, so when it happens, you sit up and take notice.

Perhaps *prophecy* is a better descriptor. I was about thirteen years old, slightly more concerned with whether a boy was going to hold my hand in the church van on the way to the Hot Hearts Conference the next weekend than I was about paying attention to the traveling preacher behind the pulpit that Sunday.

Knowing me, I was also most likely trading notes with my best friend, Jen, on the back of the church bulletin, planning and plotting until the preaching was over so we could beg our parents to take us to The Railroad Crossing restaurant, which we knew was a pipe dream because my mom definitely had a roast in the Crock-Pot, but it worked once when we were ten, so we persisted.

Jen and I snapped out of our masterminding as the traveling preacher directed the congregation's attention to the student section on the left-hand side of the sanctuary and asked all of us to stand. Our youth group of about fifty awkwardly stood, aware of every eye suddenly on us.

"These young people, right now, they are on fire for the Lord, aren't they?"

A murmur rippled through the crowd. Heads nodded. It was a Baptist church, so of course we heard an amen or two.

I don't remember the exact phrasing, but I remember the gist of what he said next. That traveling pastor pointed at all of us standing students, these future millennials with no idea what was ahead, and addressed the grown-ups of our church.

"If us believers don't start living out the real truth, if the church as a whole doesn't get its act together, if we continue to be distracted by things that don't matter, if you and I don't make Jesus Christ Lord of our lives instead of a lucky rabbit's foot, this generation of young people will get up from these pews one day and ask us what we've done with the gospel. They will walk out of this place because they know the truth doesn't live here. Church, we have the good news. It's time we act like it."

Like I said, a little bit of fortune-telling, yes?

Fast-forward thirty-some-odd years, and here we are. The data tells the story on its own. In 2021, churchgoing folks of the United States fell below the majority for the first time in our history.[1] And it's not just going to church. There's a rapid decline in those who would check the box to describe themselves as Christians at all.[2] Half of the religious demographic of "nones" left a childhood faith over a lack of belief. One in five said they "disliked" organized religion, and 18 percent indicated they are religiously unsure.[3] It's clear that traveling pastor was onto something. According to recent polls, 44 percent of people[4] will go through some kind of faith transition during their lives, and 66 percent of young people[5] who have a history of church attendance will leave by the time they are twenty-two years old. The numbers for Gen Z are even more alarming (well, depending on who you're talking to): 52 percent of young people who claim religious affiliation (and 80 percent who don't) rate their trust in religious institutions at a 4.9 on a 10-point scale.[6]

Of course, unlike this traveling pastor, it would be unfair to lay the blame entirely on our elders. If you were old enough to sit in that student section, you know we've been through a lot, personally and globally: Columbine, 9/11, the financial crisis, and COVID-19, just to name a few of our collective traumas. And, for many of us, we got kicked in the teeth by the realization that the world is quite different from church youth group, and Sunday school answers don't hold up in a hurricane of white Christian nationalism, sex abuse scandals, and the disillusionment of real life.

If the data sings the melody, then our lived experiences give this sad song its resonant harmonies. These numbers are more than just statistics; they represent flesh-and-blood children of God who feel alone, tired, and frustrated by the jarring difference between God and what cultural Christianity and partisan preachers made of "God." A lot of people today aren't exactly sure what their faith looks like, much less what it's "supposed" to look like. These masses make up the barely there believers of all ages, races, and socioeconomic statuses who are disenchanted with the expressions of the faith they were raised in.

We've been walking around with a lot of questions:

Why does an institution that claims freedom so frequently yoke its members with unnecessary burdens?

Why is there cognitive dissonance between what we read in the Gospels and the way our faith is lived out?

Why does Christianity have a reputation for hatred, big-otry, and hidden abuse?

What do you do when the church you love pretends not to notice when the vulnerable are abused?

What do you do when the church is complicit in the abuse?

Why is the church at large so obsessed with political power to the point of no longer looking like Christ?

Where is the face of Jesus Christ in the public representa-tion of faith?

Why does a faith structure that claims to be loving get so much press for doing the exact opposite?

How can I align myself with Christianity when its key message seems to revolve around exclusion?

Why is this so hard?

Is Christianity a moral good?

How do you untangle the knots of grief, anger, and pain in a place that is supposed to bear the fruit of joy, peace, and kindness?

What happens when the faith you inherited turns to ash, and how do you cope when a crisis of faith feels like an emergency?

Is this (gestures wildly) what Jesus meant? Is this, as our bracelets asked, what Jesus would do?

What, pray tell, in the actual hell is going on here?

I'm sure you have your own questions.

I don't know who you are, where you're from, or what you did (Did you sing that?), but through the work I do as the Resident Bible Scholar on the *Faith Adjacent* pod-cast and helping people disentangle faith on Beyoncé's internet, I know a lot of people are asking these types of questions. Some call it *deconstruction*, a term that's so po-larizing it means something completely different to almost everyone who uses it. Maybe you're better off calling it a faith exploration or a spiritual journey (take a drink every time you read the word *journey*); whatever it is, it can seem overwhelming, isolating, disheartening, and even shameful. Maybe it's easier just to not do all that.

And I get it. Because for a while I agreed. *Honestly, I have more than enough to keep me occupied, thanks*, I said to . . . I guess God, who I imagined perked up.

GOD
Oh. We're talking again. Hello.

ERIN
Yeah, look. I don't know if you've noticed, but it's kind oɪ a cluster here right now and I'm pretty much having an existential crisis about . . . your whole deal and our whole thing, but surely you and I can both understand I'm at capacity. Family, friends, work, community, intricate emotional and mental dynamics within all previously mentioned categories, bills to pay, appointments to schedule, humans to feed, etc. Can we table all this?

God, I imagine, did one of the things God is good at, which is be silent.

ERIN
There's no margin to breathe, much less think deep, spiritual thoughts requiring me to upend the monstrosity of a carefully constructed lifetime of faith in God—you—which would then, by its very nature, spiral into a total reconsideration of every ethic and belief I've ever held.

To which God just sustained eye contact with me while I put together what I'd just said, like that Oprah GIF where she's like, "Thank you for arriving at the conclusion. I've been here for ages."

ERIN
Okay. I get it. It's important.

I understand it's easier to ignore your doubting questions and infuriating frustrations and isolating conundrums. It's simpler to not take the risk. I'm not doing reverse psychology on you (I don't even really know how that works, I only know about it from a Baby-Sitters Club book); I know even just the act of saying you'll step into the ring can range from feeling uncomfortable to straight-up dangerous.

But underneath all that fear and unease and risk assessment is one of life's most pressing and fundamental questions. A question everyone, no matter their age or location or gender or sexuality or economic status, is faced with, usually in moments preceding great upheaval and transformation.

Do you ever feel like a plastic bag?

Posed by one of our greatest philosophers, Katy Perry, this question is really the only one worth answering before you decide if any of this faith exploration stuff is worth your time.

When you look around at your life, at the actual day-to-day, at the ways you spend your minutes and hours and days and weeks and months, do you ever feel like a plastic bag? Are you bumping along, snagging on blinding rage, snapping to unbearable sadness, getting flattened by the weight of Jesus's words versus what you see happening in the church, wallowing in a puddle of everyone else's expectations of what your life and your faith should look like? Is there somewhere in your mind or your body a recognition of a desire to stop being tossed around by who this dusty old Dutch theologian thinks is going to hell or what party this pastor thinks all Christians should be voting for? Do you want to know what your faith, your ethics, your values, your belief system would look like if you were free instead of controlled by someone or something? Do you want to be the kind of person who is so deeply convicted and innately transformed by the way they are loved by God that it permeates every minute, every hour, every day, week, month?

Katy says you just gotta ignite the light and let it shine, whatever that means. We're gonna do something different.

So, a few things from me about what this book is and what it isn't.

1. **Everyone's faith journey (drink) looks different, and I will always honor yours.** Are you going to close this book and sidle up next to me because we landed in the exact same place? No. This isn't a book that demands you end up back to being a shiny, happy Christian once again, all your questions answered and neatly tied up with a bow and a cherry on top. I don't know where you'll land or how you'll get there. Also, if you've picked up this book hoping that it contains the recipe for finalizing your own personal doctrine of faith, please contact your local bookseller and kindly request a refund. Waltzing through life thinking that faith is a fixed point we never waver from is what got us here in the first place. Your faith, no matter how it looks or where it is focused, is as alive and active as you are.

2. **I'm not the boss of you (and neither is this book).** What I'm here to do is offer up my own deconstruction/reconstruction process and share the patterns and processes I noticed, and you can take what's helpful and leave the rest.

3. **This is deeply personal work.** When I first pitched
  this book, I wanted to walk through each hot-button
  topic I'd puzzled over and show my work to the class.
  How did I become affirming? How did I arrive at an
  egalitarian interpretation of Paul's letters? How did
  my theology of hell evolve? But those were my questions, and you have your own. Your questions are for
  you, and we are not the same. You'll get some of that
  as I describe my experience, but I guess what I'm saying is you don't have to subscribe to my exact belief
  system in order to start reading this book, nor will
  you be forced to see things my way at the end.

If we can agree on those things, if we can agree the unpacking and potential repacking of your faith is complicated
and uncomfortable at best, grief-filled and agonizing even
when it's simple, maybe we can offer each other a little grace,
temper the urge to play the deconstruction suffering Olym-
pics, and allow ourselves the freedom to move at our own
pace while permitting others to do the same.

This introduction functions as a permission slip. While
you're reading this book, I invite you to box up those feelings of overwhelm, of shame, or whatever gets in your head
and heart, whispering, "This is not worth the fight." Why?
Well, here's a little spoiler. Underneath all the detritus and
debris of culture and politics and high control and toxicity,
there is something you once fell in love with.

A call of belonging.

A promise of love.

There was a moment when you were younger, either in
your mind or in your heart or in your body or all three, when
you knew or felt or heard or understood or even hoped that
something in you was treasured by Divine Love, and you

made cosmic friendship bracelets with God. I don't know how life or other people in their brokenness or even your own responsibility may have obscured that, but, for at least a moment, it was true.

That call is still there. The promise is still true. The friendship bracelet has not fallen from God's wrist. A life of honest, wrestling faith does not keep you from kinship with Jesus. Critiquing the institution of Christianity does not mean you hate it; it means you want it to be as good as it claims to be. You do not have to fall in line. You do not have to let other people's actions and beliefs determine how you will move and live and love in the world.

We don't have to let anyone walk out the door with something we love without a fight.

Here's how this is going to go down: I don't have prescriptive solutions for you, but I do have a spiritual practice to suggest—it's one that has helped me, and it's one you can make all your own.

It starts with honestly exploring where we've come from and what has shaped us.

I have come to envision my faith as a little plot of land, and the work I did there became the spiritual practice of having it out with God about . . . pretty much everything. That little plot of land is where Mark and Cindy Stewart first taught my sixth-grade Sunday school class about the parable of the lost sheep in a wood-paneled room on the third-floor annex of First Baptist Church in Canyon, Texas. It's where my mom tucked my sunflower comforter up around my chin and whispered a prayer over me before I fell asleep. That little plot of land has old standing stones, altars of faith from my grandfather and my father, established long before I was born, which will maybe one day live on someone else's land along with mine. But it's also where the uncomplicated narrative of a God who brought animals on an ark two by two to save them from a flood turned into questions about why a loving God would flood the earth and mercilessly destroy the people they* created in the first place.

So first up, you and I will spend some time reckoning with our origin stories. How did we get where we are? What brought us here? How did we become who we are and how were we shaped? We will need to start at the beginning, and we will need to survey the creations and catastrophes on our little plot of land.

When you do that, when you spend time in the past, working your way up to the present day, that process can bring with it painful perspective. Hindsight is 20/20, and it is often when we get distance that we're able to comprehend the fullness of the story that brought us to where we are today. If you're at a point of reconsidering your faith like I was, sifting through the unmet expectations and deferred dreams and broken promises will cut your knees right out from under you. And when you're on your knees, you become very good friends with grief. Because losing your faith or your community or your sense of spiritual self is a death. And while there may be a resurrection in your future, resurrections can't happen unless something dies. Or, in this case, burns. So we're going to get acquainted with the ancient practice of lament.

*Personally, I prefer using he/him pronouns when talking about God the Father, simply because it feels most natural to me. I also recognize this is an exciting time of discussion around the ways we have typically gendered the name of God. If anything, I believe God transcends gender constructs, as well as the intriguing idea that, according to the theology of the Trinity, God is three in one, effectively removing God from the concept of any kind of binary, including a gendered one, which is beyond fascinating to think about. Therefore, I have elected here to use they/them pronouns to speak of God, but I invite you to substitute whatever works best for you. If that makes you uncomfortable, I certainly understand, but it's no more outrageous to refer to the God of the Universe, embodying Divine Love, filling storehouses with snow and caring for the sparrows, as "they" than it is to refer to that God as "he." Surely that all seems rather silly anyway.

Next, I needed to lay out all my questions: the puzzles, the conundrums, the irritations, the dilemmas. You and I will walk through our spiritual inheritance and discover if our wrestling and struggling are holy or heretical.

Through that process of unpacking my questions, I had to strap on my big girl panties and look at some of my faith pressure points, those painful knots that, if we can't untangle them, render us unable to move forward. Pressure points, to me, are where our gnarliest questions come to a head and a decision point: Do we work through this and stick it out, or say, "I'm done," and leave it all behind? Of course, these pressure points will look different for everyone, but they require only one thing: clear-eyed truth, baptized in hope, which is a terrifying or liberating prospect, depending on who you ask.

When that becomes clear, you can suss out what goes and what stays. Because once you have released yourself from the need to toe any line but God's, you are free to let God be as big and wild as God wants to be in your life. This is where it got fun for me, and maybe it will for you too. I've come to understand this part of the process as pushing the boundaries of my spirituality.

I tried on new ideas, I read new authors, I tried to understand new theologies, new interpretations of Scripture. I wondered. I took a posture of curiosity. I dreamed. I stopped worrying about being called a heretic or a backslider or not a real Christian and started worrying about whether I was keeping God on a leash. I left my plot of land to go foraging to find new plant life and new seeds to bring home. What on God's earth could grow here now? I didn't collect every new thought as part of my new belief system, but I explored a new landscape where my understanding of God and faith wasn't confined by the rubber stamps of some old White men on an executive committee in Nashville.

Armed with the potential for new life, I began the work of plowing, replanting, and putting seeds in the ground and exercising a muscle I thought long atrophied: Making peace with God. Trusting things could grow again in a place that held a lot of complication.

And finally, if you keep following me, I'll show you my rewilded land. It's not perfect at all, but you already knew that. It's messy, it's still got burned-out patches, and I'm forever pulling weeds. But I'm more in love with it than I have ever been before. Whatever yours ends up looking like (again, not prescribing here!), you deserve a place that feels like home to you. And I hope this spiritual practice of having it out with God will help you create that place.

There are probably a lot of voices in your head and in your life that have an opinion about your faith journey (drink) right now. Maybe they think you're an apostate for asking questions or they say deconstruction is just an excuse for you to sin. Perhaps the call is coming from inside the house: maybe you're the one thinking you're not worthy of the process, you don't have enough time, the whole undertaking is pointless, you're going to hell for even considering some of these things, whatever they are. So, here's an invitation. Just for the time being, pack all that up. We'll deal with all those accusations, both internal and external, later. But for now, get in, loser, we're going deconstructing. Take a deep breath, step outside, and survey your own little plot of land. There are a bunch of us out here: barely there believers, outcasts wandering in a spiritual desert, and doubters standing off to the side at the church potluck. Come on. Get in here. Unless you're not a hugger—then a high five is good too.

This book is meant to walk through examining the beliefs you inherited and packed up and moved around with you your whole life. It's meant to pick up the Ebenezers of faith, turn them over in your hands, and inspect them for roots or rot. We're giving ourselves the gift of paying attention to the work of our souls, to seeing if we can make space for what once made space in us.

But first, we've got some questions. Let's ask them together.

ORIGINS

The Spiritual Strata of Our Lives
How It Started

I am a Christian because the story of Jesus is still the
story I'm willing to risk being wrong about.

Rachel Held Evans, *Inspired*

In a landfill somewhere outside of Canyon, Texas, there's a
patch of mustard-gold carpet that once graced the floors of
the First Baptist Church. If you were some kind of archae-
ologist with supernatural capabilities, you might find the
spiritual strata of my faith origins in that carpet.

You might find particles of dust from my dad's cowboy
boots as he stood next to my mother and said his marriage
vows in a gray tuxedo. Or the dried remains of sweat that
dripped from my mother's brow as she realized she was
going into labor during the third stanza of "I Surrender
All." On top of that layer is a deeply embedded piece of
fuzz from Christmas Dress 1988, a fabulous little number
from JCPenney with a plaid bow in the back, worn during

the children's choir performance of "O Little Town of Beth-lehem." You might find traces of the dirt from the bottom of my Steve Madden slip-ons carried from a mission trip in Mexico all the way back in a church van.

There might even be evidence of my baptismal meeting with Brother Jim.

"Do you accept Jesus as your personal Lord and Savior?" Sitting in the front pew, I looked Brother Jim straight in the eyes and nodded so enthusiastically my head almost bounced off my neck. Brother Jim and his wife, Patsy, were not quite old enough to be my grandparents, so they decided my brother and I would be their practice grandkids so they could get in some reps before their kids started their own families. This meant we got to sit with Patsy during church services since my mom sang in the choir and Dad was usu-ally running sound or passing the plate with the deacons. Patsy kept Certs in her purse and let us carefully peel the offering envelopes apart to draw pictures on more surface area, something Mom thought was wasteful (and to be fair, it was).

I decided to walk down the aisle to become a believer when I was about eight years old. Eight-year-old Erin loved Jesus. She didn't understand much of the Bible, and she didn't understand why we had to read stories about floods or sac-rificing your own kid in the Jesus book, but she was in. Jesus liked kids and listened to kids. He paid attention. He didn't preach a lot of long sermons; he didn't say a lot of stuff that went over a kid's head. He said if you were mean to kids, you should get thrown in the ocean, which I thought was reasonable and more people should take it seriously. Jesus seemed like a guy who wasn't worried about you getting perfect grades and wouldn't make fun of you if you didn't have the right Nikes. From what I could tell, Jesus was into snacks (fish on the beach, the Last Supper, the fishes and loaves), making sick people better, and hanging out with his friends. All things I could get down with.

Well, Jesus, and the fact that when you got baptized, they turned the lights out in the sanctuary, lit the baptistery in a very dramatic fashion, and you got to wear your swimsuit and a white robe while Brother Jim dunked you in water. And everyone watched and then amen-ed.

A crucial aspect of evangelical—specifically, Southern Baptist—culture is learning your amens. You don't know at first why someone is amen-ing something during a sermon, but you know when the lights go out and you have a water protocol, an amen is appropriate. Plus you got to skip the sermon so your mom could re-curl your hair before the invitation, which was important because basically the whole church would come and congratulate you, so you got a lot of attention. Eight-year-old Erin *so* loved attention.

But today, it was just Brother Jim and me, sitting in the front row. The main lights of the sanctuary were off, so the only light filtered in through the stained-glass windows lining the walls, bathing everything in a milky, bright glow. Brother Jim walked me through what it meant to be baptized and why it was important. At some point, the conversation pivoted to his experience in Jerusalem, where he'd seen Golgotha, the hill where Jesus is traditionally thought to have been crucified. Brother Jim was always a real one, and I remember he bought me a Butterfinger before our chat (snacks!).

"Wait. You've been there?" I asked, Butterfinger shards spilling out of my mouth.

"Yes. I got to go and see a lot of the places Jesus walked."

"Wait. Are you telling me this really happened? It's really real?"

Eight-year-old Erin was about to pledge her fealty in an ancient ceremony to this Jesus guy, but it never occurred to her that it was really, actually, hands-in-the-dirt, take-a-charter-bus-up-to-Golgotha true. The story was so good, the promises so vivid, she was willing to risk it all on the idea of it. Brother Jim went on to explain Jesus walked on the earth over two thousand years ago, he really did die, and lots of people saw him after he rose from the dead, and then he went to heaven, leaving his followers with a mandate and some teachings. He wanted to make sure I understood (as much as someone who habitually sucked on the ends of her hair could understand): This wasn't just a great story. Or rather, it was a great story, but it also happened to be true and worthy of my attention for a lot of reasons other than the snack aspect.

Brother Jim held out his hand, and slightly buried in the crease of his palm was an extremely small seed. "This is a mustard seed. Do you know anything about mustard seeds?"

I remembered a Sunday school lesson about mustard seeds, but no details emerged, so I kept eating my Butterfinger.

"Jesus said that even if you have faith as small as a mustard seed, you can move mountains. What do you think that means?"

Brother Jim is deeply good, and attempting to explain faith to an eight-year-old spitting crispety, crunchety, peanut-butteries at you should at the very least get you a hot tub in heaven. I can almost guarantee I answered, "I think it means if you want to move mountains, you only need faith that small," because I had read in the *Reader's Digest* in my grandparents' bathroom that if you don't know the answer to something, a way to sound smart was to just repeat what that person said in a different order.

Brother Jim kindly ignored the beautiful idiot in front of him and explained that all we need is the tiniest spark of faith, this minuscule seed of "What if?" and that was enough. Enough for what, I did not know then, but I would find out. I don't remember the words exactly, but I assume they went a little like, "When you get baptized, you'll go under the water and come back up. It's a way to represent that you're a new creation spiritually. You've made a promise to God that you want to love him and be loved by him. That's what happens to the mustard seed too. It gets buried and whatever it becomes can move mountains because of God's love for you and your love for him."

I still definitely thought I was supposed to be able to tele-kinetically pick up the Rocky Mountains through sheer force of will.

It seemed to me that when I entered a covenant of faith, I received a metaphorical plot of land. Not big but not small, and this was the place where God and I would be in community together, doing the holy work of trust and love. On this metaphorical plot of land, the first thing I planted was that little mustard seed. Maybe nothing noteworthy or spectacular grew, but it was something sweet and tender. Gradually, I built some buildings, complete with the same mustard-gold carpeting I knew from my home church. There was a little house, a garden, a stream, everything I needed to build a life with God and spend the rest of my time here on earth trusting that the things in the Book were true. My little plot of land was even adjacent to the land of people I loved and trusted, people who had big, shady gardens and cozy cottages they'd spent years cultivating. There was sincere warmth and courageous vulnerability, because why would you not be authentic when your authentic self is celebrated and welcomed? When I think back to that time, before the safe bubble of childhood unceremoniously popped, it rings of play, of slumber parties before girls learned we're supposed to freeze someone's bra, of curiosity holding hands with joy. I'm sure I'm romanticizing it, but it doesn't stop me from connecting with that image: me and Jesus, giggling on the trampoline, gazing at the stars. The yoke was easy, the burden was light.

I can assure you nothing magical happened the day I was baptized. I vaguely remember the gray-yellow light as the entire congregation focused on me, Brother Jim in his waders, and my mom sitting in her choir robe on the front row so she didn't have to strain her neck to look straight up at the baptistery. I assumed Brother Jim would dip me the way my mom used to rinse out my hair, making sure I didn't get my face wet, but as he dunked, he kept going until I was all the way underwater. I vaguely remember Weldon Trice shaking my hand afterward like we'd made a business deal, Treasure Brasher whispering as she gave me a hug how she'd prayed for me since I was in her nursery class, my friend Bronson sticking his tongue out at me from the back of the line. I remember Patsy telling me I made an outward sign of an inward change, that Jesus came into my heart, and that I was a new creation. There was that phrase again. I wondered if New Creation Erin would still color-sort her Skittles while she watched *The Flintstones*. Would she be nicer to her little brother? Would she cease complaining about picking up dog poop in the backyard? What was Jesus doing in my heart? The same thing the mustard seed was doing? If this was supposed to symbolize an inward change, how was I changing and how could I tell?

As my own timeline moved away from that moment with Brother Jim on the front row, I began to evaluate what belonged on my plot of land. Of course, I was eight, so at first there wasn't a lot of introspection. And let's be frank, there wasn't a lot of introspection until I got to my thirties. That is (1) a part of my personality, (2) a survival technique, and (3) fear, all of which we'll get to. So what ended up built or planted on my plot of land were either the kinds of truths you'd confidently utter standing eye-to-eye with the devil himself or lies dressed up so cleverly as truths, you might confidently utter them as well. And, for me, it was hard to tell the difference.

I didn't ask anyone about this. It would take another thirty-two years (and counting) for that Erin to understand that yes, the idea of Jesus is excellent, no notes, but the reality of following Jesus is a cluster of epic proportions.

My very own New Creation hands would build altars to legalism, construct tabernacles to purity culture, and stubbornly refuse to pull up the thorny weeds of performing faith for an audience that choked out an actual, blood-rich, heart-pumping life with God. I would make a failed run at being a missionary, convinced I could force my way back into God's good graces, and at the same time convinced I was doing God a favor. I watched as people I trusted planted invasive vegetation on my land, and I got so attached to those weeds I started to care for them myself, tender mustard seeds be damned. Vines of smug superiority attached themselves to every building, and in the face of honest questions, I observed as those carefully constructed facades crumbled, unable to carry the weight. Pollutants from upstream—leadership failures, *Access Hollywood* tapes, white Christian fascism that pitted *us* against *them*, a special brand of religious misogyny where everyone is just really nervous about breasts, and a global pandemic where a lot of American evangelicals showed their asses—seeped into the soil, withering the garden and rotting the foundations.

And of course, there I was: broken, angry, and leaning into every irate impulse to judge and rage and point fingers. I didn't ask anyone about the inward change because I could see their outward signs. I could see my outward signs, and they were not great. I'd heard a billion sermons about how Christians are supposed to be set apart, how God is love, and how "the world" would know us by this love, and frankly, I saw some discrepancies with me and with everyone. Suddenly I belonged nowhere. My own culpability collided head-on with the landslide of cultural Christianity-lite, smothering everything that once lived and thrived on that little plot of land eight-year-old Erin and Jesus once giggled on.

Even the cornerstones I thought I could rely on showed signs of decay: the inerrancy of Scripture, the Trinity, heaven, hell, the person of Jesus himself. I could barely look at all the things I thought I was certain about, because if I did, I was paralyzed with fear that it would not sustain my gaze and everything I built my life on was pure and utter bullshit. And while that wasn't a reason that it couldn't be true, it wasn't something I was prepared to unpack. Until not unpacking it was worse than keeping it packed.

The soil was toxic, the air was poisonous, and not one thing could live, much less grow.

To sum it up, my plot of land was overgrown in all the wrong places and dead where green things were meant to grow. That mustard seed of faith now felt like a downright luxury.

This, of course, was me. But I know I was not and am not alone in this. Swap out some of the details, the timelines, the characters, and perhaps you're nodding your head right along with me. We'd know one another just by the look of unbelonging ghosting around us. Home was not (or is not) home anymore.

I've always scored high in the Faith category on the Spiritual Giftings test, which is ironic considering I wish someone would tell me what faith means. Whoever wrote the book of Hebrews reminds us that faith is "confidence in what we hope for and assurance about what we do not see" (11:1 NIV), which is obtuse at best. You cannot have the assurance of something you hope for. Hope is not a game plan. By its very nature hope is nebulous, so you cannot be assured of it at all.

I know I have faith in things, but they are things I know will happen, not the things I hope for. The sun will rise, right? I know that because science and Neil deGrasse Tyson say so. I have faith in my marriage, yes, because my husband and I trust each other, but also because we are very tired and the thought of locking someone else down is something we've mutually agreed sounds exhausting.

And there are things I once had faith in, and now I'm not so sure. I don't know how to have faith in humanity at large (sorry! I was traumatized by a global pandemic where half the population was convinced it was a conspiracy theory!), but sometimes small tender moments of authentic humanization flit across my vision and I'm reminded that there is still real warmth in the world.

I used to have a lot of faith in the church (sorry! I lived through too many denominations covering up too many sexual abuse scandals!), but sometimes I walk into my scrappy little Sunday school class and I'm reminded that not everyone is a part of the problem.

I used to have faith in my interpretation of the Bible (sorry! I've lived just long enough to regret my substitutionary-atonement era of fangirling over John Piper!), but sometimes

I'll read a brilliant thinker unpacking Scripture in a way that speaks to my soul, and I'll reconsider throwing it all out.

Faith can feel hurried, as if we're trying to finish building the airplane as we're taxiing down the runway. It can feel alien, like a family heirloom that's been handed down for generations and you don't exactly know how to incorporate it into your current life. Faith ebbs and flows: sometimes you are connected and spiritually nourished, and sometimes you very much would like to be excluded from this narrative. All around us people are deconstructing and reconstructing (or not), and everyone seems to have an opinion about the merits or demerits of that process. Our faiths get tangled up with the faiths of our people— parents, grandparents, partners, friends, kids, coworkers, and culture—to the point where we're not sure where they end and we begin.

We have a lot of examples of what "bad faith" looks like because it's often bombastic, absurd, and loud. In fact, bad faith looks a lot like fear, a way to either insulate yourself from the things that scare you or blow up like a freaked-out porcupine so no one else knows how scared you are.

The Latin for "bad faith" is *mala fides*, and it means "with intent to deceive." Agents of mala fides often obfuscate and bury inconvenient truths, whether that's a line item on the church budget or knowledge of their personal offenses that would disqualify them from holding any kind of leadership position (in an ideal world, anyway). Agents of mala fides have junior officers that work with them to deceive for power, money, and authority. Headlines keep us up-to-date on all the current workings of these agents of mala fides, and there is no shortage of the pain and disappointment they bring along with them.

You could probably guess this, but the opposite of *mala fides* is *bona fides*: "good faith." Many of us know the modern usage of this phrase to mean evidence of qualifications: degrees, certificates, and diplomas that prove someone is who they say they are. But if you take it back to the original Latin, *bona fides* simply means "genuinely, or with sincerity."

While we have a lot of examples of mala fides, bona fides is a little more difficult to find. That's because it's quieter, it's not showy, it can't be contained in a sound bite or a reel. Developing bona fides is slow and deliberate. It's not linear; it's more circular because it's not a race or a destination. It's almost never certain, but it is curious. It's not clickable or a step-by-step process, but if I'm honest, I don't really know what having faith is supposed to mean, concretely. I think part of it is engaging questions with sincerity, and not deceiving yourself with thinking you have all the answers. I have faith in Jesus, which means I've never met Jesus physically but I have met him personally, which I acknowledge is a puzzling thing to say. And not only that, but I also believe he loves me. When you type it out like that, it really is something that objectively can make you seem a little weird.

I have no idea if the plans for my life are to prosper me and not to harm me, or if they're just a random string of occurrences I've placed a religious boundary around to make myself feel better about hurtling toward the abyss that will accompany my death. I claim a certain set of beliefs within the tiny sliver of the Christian tradition I occupy, and I dump on everyone who doesn't fit within my very narrow scope of understanding, probably to make myself feel better about maybe not being correct.

To add another layer, I'm a parent, and everyone tells me I'm supposed to be nurturing my children's faith. In this economy? I don't even know what I believe in anymore, and you want me to guide these tiny people? In the Lord?! I can't stop pinching their chunky thighs in their car seat buckle; I don't think I should be trusted with spiritual formation.

Am I deconstructing? Is asking a question or two about the way this whole thing is set up deconstructing? Is deconstructing bad? Do I care? Wow, okay some people *do not* like this deconstruction thing. Do I want to reconstruct? What will that look like? What if that guy I'm married to / the father of my children doesn't see things as I do anymore? What do I think about inerrancy and hell and affirming theology and women in leadership and on and on and on until I'm buried in a morass of social issues and faith problems and searching for God—but wait, someone put the empty milk jug back in the fridge, and I don't have space to think about anything, much less weighty matters of spirituality that seem to be on a timer that dings with finality at the end of my life, and I hope you're happy with your choices because they are forever and one is cool, with gold mansions and fat baby angels, and the other is decidedly not, with fiery lakes of eternal torture, so figure it out!

So I was at a crossroads, feeling like a plastic bag. Maybe you've been there as well; it's possible you're there right now. And the thing about growing up religious, the thing about being pickled in the brine of religion is you hear and absorb things so deeply, you almost forget they have the potential to not be true. You live so long in a religious structure you forget you signed up for a way of living that defies the physical world in a way that doesn't make logical sense. You forget you once giggled under the stars with a God who supposedly didn't stay dead. If that is the case, what's to stop that God from bringing a dead faith back to life? What's to stop that God from walking with you through a process where you try to figure out what's real

and true, what's baggage and bullhonky?* What's to stop
that Holy Spirit from making all things new, including you?
If we really truly believe Jesus is who he says he is, then let's
dance, you know?

But my plot of land was thick with sickness, overgrowth,
and disease. I didn't know where to begin and I didn't know
if I would end up in a place anyone, including myself, would
like. I have always been haunted by a quote misattributed to
Carl Sagan: "If it can be destroyed by the truth, it deserves to
be destroyed by the truth." What if the process of finding out
what's real and true leads to a place I've never been before?
What if I am an enormous chicken who is too attached to
her comfort rituals to face the truth? Who am I underneath
all this and who is God and what am I supposed to be cultivating on this little plot of land?

At the beginning of my disentangling, I came across an
article about controlled burning, or prescribed fire. Wildfires
have always been a part of my life, growing up in West Texas.
It's one of the driest parts of the country, covered in acres of
crispy grass that can easily burn the length of three football
fields every second. Every male I grew up with has some
version of a story where they almost caused or did cause a
wildfire. But something that many West Texas ranchers, like
my family, will do is set a controlled burn before a wildfire
has a chance to go to town on life, limb, and livestock. Plus,
any weekend is made inherently great to a ten-year-old by
starting a fire from the back of a pickup truck, I don't care
who you are.

---

*Watch me get progressively more desperate to find a creative replacement for
"bullshit" now that I've availed myself of my one free allotted use. When you see
one of these ridiculous words, please know what I'm really saying is "bullshit"—
unfortunately it IS the finest descriptor, so crisp and evocative—but my publisher,
whom I greatly respect, has asked me to rein it in. But you and I both know what
I mean. These two didn't count because they're in the footnotes. See? Creativity!

While I thought we were just enjoying a casual forty-eight hours as freelance arsonists, a controlled burn actually has an important purpose. It's a tactic used by Indigenous peoples and forestry scientists to maintain the health of the land: a low-intensity fire is started intentionally to clear out overgrowth that might otherwise spark a high-intensity, out-of-control fire later. In other words, it is a fire set not toward destruction, but toward purposeful renewal. It burns the brush, the weeds, the plants at risk of causing a true wildfire that will destroy everything, and it transfigures all of this into rich fertilizer that will support new life in its place. It doesn't leave the health of the area to chance. It takes it seriously—so seriously in fact, it's willing to set the damn place on fire.

Something in me was itching to light a match and let fire do what fire does: purify what's true and burn the bullshit* to nothing. I wanted to drop an A-bomb on the mess that was my faith and see what remained, if anything. What could possibly grow again? I could either spend the rest of my life in service to a thin version of a weak God who worked only in the suburbs of America and didn't align with anything I read about, or I could take the one I saw in Scripture at God's word and see if God meant what God said about untying the ropes of death and how we have a home in God forever.

So I poured the gasoline. I struck the match and put it to the edge of the property line. And it all just lit right up, the flames and the heat and the burning and the fireworks.

I mean, it wasn't that dramatic. It was a metaphorical fire, but it definitely felt that dramatic.

*Look, my editor GAVE me that one just for the purpose of alliteration. A bonus!

44

What followed the Great Fire was a messy and imperfect process of fits and starts, of fear and trembling, of learning and unlearning, that slowly morphed into the book you're holding now in your hands. There was lament, weeping, and gnashing of teeth. There was a time of intense questioning, a real *Law and Order: SVU* situation, laying it all out for examination. I had to take an honest look at where my faith or lack thereof was under pressure and come to terms about whether I could be okay in that pressure. There were moments and issues I had to make real peace with, an active peacemaking that continues daily. I got theologically promiscuous and flirted with some doctrines that would have made eighteen-year-old me start pumping out the holy water for an exorcism. And I ultimately had to ask myself what it looked like to rewild my land, and did I even want it anymore?

Within the pages of this book, I hope you'll find less of a "Deconstruct Your Faith in Six Weeks!" course* and more of a friend who's been there, is kind of still there, and is happy to wander over to your plot of land while it's in whatever stage of smoldering to offer a potential next step or just a hug or a cookie. I hope we can walk together, wading through the ash and detritus of what we've set on fire to see what gets to stay, what gets thanked for its service but needs to go, and what gets the middle finger while you watch its embers blow away forever.

We might be in different stages of the process. Maybe your garden is healthier than mine, or maybe you're wearing a hazmat suit to detoxify your soil. You might still be wondering if you can strike that match. I get it. Even if you're on the fence about it, what I hope you leave with at the end of our time together is the hope that even when you've let that

*That should not exist, and if you ever see it in the wild, run away. Run far away.

blaze rage, you're not alone and you have permission to own your spiritual life. It is yours, and at the end, you're the only one who must answer for it. You don't have to follow the prescription laid out for you, even by me. You bought this book, but you don't have to listen to me.

You feel alone because any deviation from the norm is designed to make you feel alone,* but our history of faith is crowded with pioneers who lit their own matches and tried again with God. Folks like Julian of Norwich, Bernard of Clairvaux, St. Therese, and James Baldwin: these humans experienced God in a way that didn't line up with the way they were taught, with the way culture and life told them it should, and they said, "Nope. Burn it down and let's see what's under all this applesauce."† Our faith history is full of events where groups of people did the same, some we know, some which have been hidden or repackaged so as not to give us any funny ideas about our own freedom.

What you'll see when you blowtorch your own section of land is that when night comes, there are bonfires everywhere. There are a lot of us out here, cobbling together what we know of God, of Jesus, of Holy Spirit, of faith, of love, of hope, rebuilding in a new way with a cornerstone inherited from long ago. This book is for you if you're overwhelmed and wandering and unsure, if you're wondering why the faith you've nurtured doesn't line up with what you've heard about Jesus, and if you've wondered whether any of it is worth keeping. Let's give ourselves the gift of paying attention to the work of our souls. We don't have to feel like a plastic bag. If the thought of that makes you want to turtle up into

*It's a feature, not a bug.
†This is a fun way to tell you I just discovered "applesauce" is a synonym for BS.

a nap forever, that's okay too. Doubts, exhaustion, frustration, and hanging on by a thread are extremely welcome here.

I don't know where you were coming from when you picked up this book. It's possible your deconstruction story will end with you deconstructing yourself right out of faith. I have met enough people with enough deep-down religious trauma, I have seen enough of the pain my own religion has caused, I have been the perpetrator of pain within the context of that religion to know that deconverting is the only way some people can survive. Given the stories I have heard of abuse, racism, and misogyny within the walls of the church, some people must get out of the business of faith to stay alive. If that is you, I get it. I really do. I won't attempt to gaslight you into staying. I won't shame you or tell you passive-aggressively that I'll pray for you. If nothing else, I hope someone has seen and witnessed you and your very real suffering, and if not, I am sorry. I don't know if me tangentially saying I see you through these pages matters, but I really do. It sucks, and I'm so sorry.

But if you're interested in trying it out, in setting it on fire and seeing what remains, let's rage. I think you'll resonate with these pages if you're the kind of person who constantly feels the tension of what Jesus *said* and what his people *do*. Who thrashes around in the cognitive dissonance of loving the sinner and hating the sin. Who isn't sure about inerrancy but loves the Bible while also being weirded out by it. Who is weirded out by the Bible but can really get on board with Jesus. Who is also sometimes extremely puzzled and even annoyed by Jesus. Who doesn't feel like there's any time to sort any of it out, so they just continue to live, frustrated by the attempt to reconcile a good faith in a world that seems to only applaud a bad one, plastic bagging it day by day.

It's good for me to go back to my spiritual strata, to remember those Butterfinger shards and that mustard seed cradled in Brother Jim's palm. Because I think for a long time I thought Jesus was putting the burden of faith on us.

JESUS

You ding-dong. I know you're too stupid and ill-equipped to do anything, you big dumb moron, so if you can just manage to scrape together the tiniest amount of faith, I will condescend to deal with you. Your faith can "move mountains," which in this case, I mean it can keep you locked in a cycle of never praying hard enough, always simultaneously being too much and not enough, thinking it's possible to earn my love while knowing you've screwed up too much for it. You'll be constantly frustrated, perpetually anxious, and everyone will say the reason is because your faith is too small, even though I told you it was enough. Hahahaha, gotcha.

But I think maybe that was other interpretations and understandings coloring my perspective of who was responsible for what in this mustard seed transaction. Because when I look back at the mustard seed story, it's nestled within some interesting context.

Jesus and a few of his besties have just come off a wild experience called the transfiguration. For the uninitiated, the transfiguration is when Jesus, Peter, James, and John went to the top of a mountain and Jesus—wait for it—transfigured in front of them. Basically, it was a moment for him to show them what that fully God thang do in a fully human context: light emanating from his person, his clothes taking on supernatural whiteness, some Old Testament characters popping in to mix it up. If they had any doubts about Jesus being who he hinted at being, well, I'd be pretty convinced if I saw him having a casual chat with Moses, who had definitely been dead for a few millennia at this point.

But when Jesus and the disciples come down off the mountain, they are greeted by a man who begs for his son to be healed. He wants Jesus to do it because the disciples can't, which, how embarrassing, right? Jesus makes short order of the boy's healing, and later, when the disciples have Jesus to themselves, they ask him why they couldn't do it.

Most English translations give his answer as some form of "because you have little faith" or "because of your unbelief" or "because you don't have enough faith" or "because you don't trust enough." And these all get the idea across, but I think I prefer the way The Message puts it: "Because you're not yet taking *God* seriously" (Matt. 17:20, italics in the original). Imagine telling a group of people who just saw the second person of the Trinity enfleshed in his glory while he talked to a guy taken to heaven in a chariot driven by angels that they don't take God seriously.

I had, like many of us do, conflated a strong faith with taking God seriously. I had a very strong faith. To most people and even to myself, it wasn't any more complicated than I did the right things, said the right things, believed the right things, and therefore my version of strong faith was passable. But what's the point in having faith, strong or otherwise, in a God of applesauce, bullhonkey, and malarkey?

Taking God seriously is a whole other matter altogether. You bring the mustard seed, God brings God, in all God's banana-pants liberation and annoying insistence on loving enemies and bone-deep belonging and radical hospitality.

But it would be a while before those pieces clicked into place for me, and it would even be a while before I began thinking Jesus considered me a big, dumb moron.

For now, it was just me and my friend Jesus, watching the soil for any sign of a green shoot poking through the earth, the first thing we ever planted on that little plot of land, never dreaming that one day we'd be watching this whole thing burn to the ground. But I'm glad I didn't know, because I think I would have assumed burning it down would be the death of me.

Now I know striking the match feels like it might kill you, but it won't. The only thing that will kill you is pretending everything is okay when it's not.

Like a Wrecking Ball

How It's Going

> Most theology, like most fiction, is essentially autobiographical.
>
> Frederick Buechner, *The Alphabet of Grace*

My spiritual upbringing gave me bread. It also gave me snakes. It's taken me a long time to come to terms with both those things being true.

I can't speak for everyone's experience, but here's what mine was like: I hold sacred space in my heart for fellowship hall potlucks and Vacation Bible School and early morning Bible studies over breakfast burritos. My heroes were Cassie Bernall, Valeen Schnurr, and Rachel Scott, three students shot during the Columbine massacre for reportedly refusing to renounce their faith in God in the face of death. I spent hours in my Teen Life Application Study Bible, secretly lingering on the special glossy pages about sex or the temples or the end times, all hot-button topics for Young Erin. I carefully made a point of thinking about the rapture every day, whispering under my breath, "Today's the day!" just in case God decided today *was* the day, so I could thwart God and remain firmly planted on earth until someone wanted to court me / kiss dating goodbye with me, then marry me, then have sex with me, in that order, obviously. I would not go to glory a virgin, because no matter what my youth pastor said about heaven, there was no way singing in a cloud forever was better than sex.*

And then college happened, and I could make my faith my own, but also: boys and alcohol. Because I really liked the social currency of being a top-tier Christian and the fun of the boys and the alcohol, I thought, *Why not do both?* This is how I was serving on the university leadership team at my church and showing up hungover on Sunday mornings. That verse about "Do not let your left hand know what your right hand is doing"? Nailed it. But that wasn't sustainable, so when I went to work for a para-church ministry over the summer, God, as the early aughts pastors used to say, "got ahold of my life," and the pendulum swung from boys and alcohol to legalism and John Piper.

There were threads that ran through this performance of faith in all its iterations. On my little plot of land, I needed to show God, myself, and everyone else that I was DOING THE THING. And what better way to do that than build a little theater on my land? It would provide shelter to allow me to continue my religious tap dance performance indefinitely, while nodding to the fact that I am dramatic as hell.

The wise woman builds her (play)house upon the rock, obviously, but she needs something with which to build. So I took what I understood about the concept of faith—that I

*I still maintain this is true, although my theologies of both heaven and sex have evolved considerably.

needed to stage a production of it, a little song-and-dance, to show everyone what I was about—and started to build on my land.

Growing up in evangelical culture, particularly in the '80s and '90s, we were big into Box Checking Culture. I love a to-do list, some goal setting, a docket, so this spoke to me. And when you checked a box back then, you received a reward in the form of building materials, to extend our little plot of land metaphor. Allow me to explain.

Let's say you read your Bible today. Box checked; you may now gather some wood.

Did you tithe 10 percent of your allowance? Check the box. Here are some bricks.

Were you actively not mean to the kid in Spanish class who is probably gay? Check. Here are some shingles.

Did you vote Republican? Here's some insulation.

Did you and your boyfriend ask for forgiveness after what happened in the back seat of his truck? Whew. That was a close one. Please take these stage lights and do better.

Were you so brave and did you raise your hands during the worship service? Or were you super brave and did you stand up before everyone else? Wow. Take a curtain, my sister in Christ.

Did you ever question if the book of Revelation wasn't literally true? No? Good. Why in the world would this insane fever dream on the island of Patmos not be a metaphor for Roman rule?

Girls are supposed to be quiet and not teach or preach? Okay. It says it right here, so I guess that's it.

I did not question authority, I did not examine my beliefs, I did not prosecute or press or wonder. I just lived in this safe bubble, doing my little tap dance, happily following every detail in the construction manual.

And some of that is completely developmentally appropriate. I'm too old and I've done too much work to flagellate myself for what I did when I was trying in earnest. Yes, the primordial goo of my faith journey (drink) was rooted in performance, but I also know I would not perform something I didn't care about. Somewhere underneath my hope to go full Song of Songs with a boy before the rapture or my fervent belief that only Republicans could go to the good place, I know I was responding to a call to put the stupid hammer down. To stop all this hornswoggle and just be beloved. And I think I was trying. But even when you're trying, you can still fudge it up.

And the thing about performing faith, or as it's widely known, legalism, is that it really does serve you just fine if absolutely nothing bad ever happens in your life. If the house you built with legalism is never tested, you don't have anything to worry your sweet little head about. If you never have to question or doubt your faith, those bricks and lumber and nails will hold up just fine. You won't even need to have the inspector come out.

If tragedy never strikes, performative faith will serve you just fine.

If no one ever disappoints you, it's fine.

If you're never confronted with new information, it's fine.

Because you're not actually taking God seriously, you're taking yourself seriously. You have faith in your performance, and God really doesn't have much to do with it.

But none of us are spared the full spectrum of life. Some of us more than others, but life in all its lifey-ness certainly comes for us all.

And it doesn't even matter how that crucible, that trial, that kneecapping comes. It can be as simple as an offhand comment or as complex as learning about how we got the

Holy Scriptures. It can be as quick as an election day or as slow as someone dying of a terminal disease. It can come from friend or foe, in youth or old age. Whatever it is that rides in is not there to test the strength of your building, but there is a testing anyway.

You become aware of wood splintering, roofs caving in, fires breaking out, foundations cracking. Everything you thought was going to hold you up or keep you safe turns out to be as substantial as a fart in the wind.

You cannot perform faith when there is no stage.

You can't yet know that the doubt accompanying this testing is a gift. It's not possible to comprehend the invitation being extended to you: to take God seriously, at God's word. There's no way to see at the beginning what thirteenth-century Christian mystic and English anchoress Julian of Norwich saw: "First the fall, and then the recovery from the fall, and both are the mercy of God."[1]

All you know right now is that the rug's been pulled out from under you. What was solid is now shifting, what was sturdy is now wobbling. And look, some of us are pros at pretending we're fine. *This is definitely not shifting; what are you talking about? Wobbly? I'm not wobbly. You must be wobbly. Worry about yourself.* And we push the fear down and attempt to ignore it or hide from it, which pressurizes the confusion, and soon you're sitting on a tinderbox with a stick of dynamite and a match.

And it's not like we're very good at helping each other through it. Sometimes maybe you land on a magical unicorn of a family or a friend group who will midwife you through this era of doubt and frustration and sorrow and anger. But one of the worst parts is there might be people you love who walk among your rubble and use those splinters and shards of glass as weapons to make themselves feel better.

Looks like your house wasn't built on the Lord.
Sounds like you're capitulating to the world.
You probably weren't even a Christian in the first place.
Doesn't seem like your faith was all that strong to begin
with.

You don't say. And, amazingly, you begin to see that's the whole point. You did all these things you were told would save your soul and make you nice and palatable and a part of something, but when every single thing in your life fell apart, not one brick held up.

Suddenly, the places where you felt safe are no longer trustworthy. The people who embedded the stories of God in you turned out not to believe their own press. The prayer you've prayed for years remains stubbornly unanswered or falls flat. The way believers wield and weaponize the Lord's name sickens you. The scandal of the gospel made small and weak, Americanized and commodified, a thin gruel that nourishes no one. Not only that, but you know your own heart. You know the ways you've jazz-handed your way into propping up this religion, you know the ways you've been complicit. The more you look at the big picture, sitting there amid your own rubble, the more you want to set the whole thing ablaze.

And I think this is good. There's a clarity that comes with cleaning house. Because what good is a religion uninspected? What good are questions left unprosecuted? What is the point of a faith that does nothing, means nothing, changes nothing, resurrects nothing?

There will come a moment when the cost of stasis becomes greater than the cost of change. You'll realize nothing could be worse than keeping up a facade that says, "Everything is fine." You'll stop ignoring the voice, the hints, the questions, and the thoughts that invade your mind and heart. You'll get brave and stand up from the wreckage of whatever you've built and grown on your plot of land. You'll hack through the overgrowth and the thorns and say a little prayer under your breath: "Let's see what you've got."

And you will set the whole thing ablaze. You won't get struck by lightning; you will light it up yourself.

There is a time to be gentle, and there is a time to be ruthless. Whatever it is that haunts you about your faith, there will not be peace for you until you give yourself over to examining it. Maybe it's time to ruthlessly survey the damage on your little plot of land and decide what's next.

There's no formula for deconstruction. It's a death to mourn, but there's no funeral. It's a journey (drink) to take, but there's no road. It's a prayer to stumble through, but there's no liturgy. What I've learned, though, is that you can start by going back to your personal beginnings. You might as well examine your origin story, asking yourself how you got there, who it made you into, and the differences between the snakes and the bread.

Some of that will require looking at people you love and admitting they did their best, but failed you. Some people, it will be hard to admit, did their best and it simply was not good enough. You will be challenged to look into the mirror and pay attention to the ways you were or are part of the problem. It will mean being honest about your fury, your collusion, your ache, your questions. You'll need to decide if you want to be part of the solution. As a non-introspective person, trust me, I know this makes some of you want to die. It makes me want to die.

But I know what it's like to walk around with that death in my heart, acting like everything is just fine, thanks. I know what it's like when the Lexapro works for your brain but doesn't reach your spirit. I understand the way it feels when the things that stirred your heart in love for the Divine make you want to grit your teeth so hard, they break. Eking out a life while trying to coexist with that death is not sustainable. We either rage against the dying of the light or we carefully paper over the destruction, hoping no one will see the cracks. But we can face the reckoning head-on, because, as Anne Lamott says, "You can't get to any of these truths by sitting in a field smiling beatifically, avoiding your anger and damage and grief. Your anger and damage and grief are the way to the truth. We don't have much truth to express unless we have gone into those rooms and closets and woods and abysses that we were told not to go in to."[2] Again, I hate it just as much as you might. And the worst part is, this is your process. It's not something anyone can do for you. Sure, this book gives you a framework, and sure, I'm here to hold your hand in a metaphorical sense if you want me to, but this is between you and God.

And if it's going to be your process, your road, your liturgy, there are some things to consider. Your upbringing doesn't look like mine. Your faith heritage doesn't look like mine. You don't experience God in the same ways I might. Your doubts and questions are not mine. We don't share the same joys and disappointments in our spiritual lives. We don't wrestle with the same problems, and the thoughts that plague me may not bother you at all. The people who hurt me may have been the ones who helped you hang on for dear life. That is what makes this season, this process, so deeply personal, and why this cannot just be a rote exercise that promises results at the end of the book. Where we came from is different and where we're headed might be as well.

And as much as I want to nudge you to the same spot where I landed, I know that would be manipulative, and I'm retired from that job. But ending up someplace means we start somewhere, and knowing where we're from, how we were forged, and who helped make us who we are will go a long way in understanding what deserves to get regrown and rewilded on our little plot of land later.

I want to be clear that no transformation, however positive, however necessary, feels good in the moment. We're not tweaking or recalibrating; we're overthrowing an insidious regime bent on keeping us complacent, too busy to do anything about it, and too overwhelmed to figure out how to change it. That's why I'm drawn to the metaphor of setting it all on fire. You will feel the heat, taste the ash, and maybe experience the slow microscopic push of new, green life being born out of something dead, because with every atom I am made of, I believe when someone seeks truth, they do not come up empty-handed.

But it also sometimes feels like trying, attempting, giving something a shot, earnestly making an effort is vulnerable work because what if nothing happens? What if you put yourself out there and you get stood up or rejected? That moment of walking off the stage, removing all the makeup, hanging up the costumes, and emerging as just plain old you is authentically terrifying, especially after you've experienced hurt at the hands of religion. And asking for connection? Just rip my heart out and let's let everyone watch it bleed and twitch on the sidewalk, shall we? Misery.

But this Jesus guy says if we seek, we will find. He says if we knock, the door will be open to us. He says we can ask. So if you're comfortable with it, ask. Maybe it feels silly or trite. Maybe it pisses you off to even have to ask, and I get that. But if you want, ask. Ask for God to show the hell up during this process. Ask for eyes to see and ears to hear. Ask for an open heart and a sharp mind. Ask for God to be with you, and for you to know it. Ask to experience God's love.

Ask for a spirit that can fully embody what it means to be resurrected.

Fr. Richard Rohr says that "we tend to see [resurrection] only in the long run. In the short run, it often just looks like death."[3] Could real life be worth a death? Is this one life you're gifted with worth the chance to really see if the wild stories and unreal promises and impossible standards and upside-down kingdom are true? And if they are, wouldn't they be deserving of more than just a nominal place in your life? What would have to die, what would need to get wrecked, in order for the thin belief system to go up in smoke and something with teeth to be born in its place?

The only things that end up dying are the things that really didn't deserve to flourish in the first place. Of course, we can't see that on this side. And first, we've got to do something with all these ashes.

LAMENT

White Lion Hot Dog Jonathan Jesus

If you have not learned to lament, you have not learned to love. To love someone is to know and be known, which means opening oneself up to the possibility of being hurt by another.

Jemar Tisby, *How to Fight Racism*

I do not like The Sads.

Grief, for me, is best processed with several orders of Sonic chili cheese fries. That's it. I'm a very simple person. When someone dies, allow me to make a casserole with various creams. You need me to sit with you during chemo? Look at this fine collection of memes I've curated for you instead. You are heartbroken over a boy? You responsibly take shots and then I'll drive us by his house with our middle fingers up right when the good part of the Olivia Rodrigo song comes on and then we'll play *Mario Kart* and pretend to run him over.

So, you could say I don't handle The Sads well. OR that I am handling them amazingly.

But I am an adult who goes to therapy, and I knew if I was going to start to process this whole deconstruction thing, I needed to pay attention to the ways I was devastatingly sad about my faith and everything surrounding it. And because I didn't want to look directly at my own sadness, I thought looking at it indirectly through the lens of science was the ticket. I am a child of the '90s, brought up by *Bill Nye the Science Guy*, after all.

About ten years ago, my grandfather died. My Papa was (is) larger than life, a West Texas rancher who quoted Shakespeare and was once almost gored to death by a bull. He was ornery and secretly a softie, and his death was like a crater in our family. I wasn't fully able to grasp the way his death reoriented our lives until I read *The Grieving Brain: The Surprising Science of How We Learn from Love and Loss* by Mary-Frances O'Connor.* In it, she makes the case that grief is a relearning, a process by which a person rebuilds their life around the loss of another person. It's not that they ever really move on, they just relearn and adjust how they live without them. She says, "Grief is a heart-wrenchingly painful problem for the brain to solve, and grieving necessitates learning to live in the world with the absence of someone you love deeply, who is ingrained in your understanding of the world. This means that for the brain, your loved one is simultaneously gone and also everlasting, and you are walking through two worlds at the same time. You are navigating your life despite the fact that they have been stolen from you, a premise that makes no sense, and that is both confusing and upsetting."[1]

For many people who grew up in a Christian culture of some kind who now feel homeless within that same culture, that type of grief is recognizable. Two worlds at the same

*Please ignore that O'Connor's book came out almost a decade after my Papa's death; I am a chronically slow processor.

time? We get it. We aren't learning how to live without a person necessarily, but we're learning how to live without the same systems and answers we've used our entire lives, and anyone who's gone through it will tell you it is a death. "Gone and also everlasting" is deeply apt for those of us who live with these varying degrees of developmental religious trauma. The scaffolding that bound us in a community, certainty to ease our mind, and clear assurances that we are right and being right makes us safe are pulled out from under our feet, and we are, to put it lightly, unmoored.

Not only are we unmoored, but we are also isolated. Maybe we speak up about a small thing not sitting right with us and no one else in the group relates (or at least they aren't brave enough or safe enough at the moment to relate out loud), so we sink further into that isolation, that sense of "What's wrong with me? Everyone else seems to be just fine with the way things are, so why am I so bothered?" And the feeling of loneliness might not just be in our friend groups and Sunday school classes, but prevalent in our own homes.

No wonder we're grieving when the Sunday school teacher who pulled out the felt board and poured the Kool-Aid for snack time starts spouting on Facebook that a certain presidential candidate is God's literal chosen one.

No wonder we're grieving when we read about how tax-exempt megachurches use their fat budgets to line their pockets instead of feeding the poor or making their buildings ADA-compliant.

No wonder we're grieving when we see that one conspiracy theorist pastor's book on our parents' nightstand.

And of course, it's not just the manifestation of whatever dog-and-pony show is happening here in American churches or in our own homes, it's also actual faith. It's the actual Bible. It's the person of Jesus. You sit in Sunday school as a kid, hearing about how Jesus was sinless and perfect, and through all the stories you read in the Gospels, that seems to ring true. You can finagle the whipping frenzy in the temple into righteous anger: yeah, you can see it. And then you start reading the Gospels on your own and you come to a story you've never read before where Jesus calls a lady a . . . dog? What's that now? What's going on with our guy? Did someone just stick that in the Bible when we weren't looking, or has it been there all along?

And what about the Bible, anyway? We were sold the doctrine of inerrancy, that the Bible was the perfect, inerrant word of God, only to learn that's a concept made up by a bunch of guys in the '70s. Not the 1270s. Not the 1670s. The 1970s.* The Bible is a manual for how to live our lives. What does the Bible have to say about artificial intelligence or climate change or school shootings? What about the ways the Bible contradicts itself? What does it actually have to do with our real, lived lives?

What about the problem of evil? Why would a good and all-powerful God let all of this (*gestures wildly*) go unchecked? If there's a God, that God must be a moral monster to allow all this injustice and all this cruelty to triumph in the world. The abuses done to humanity in the name of this particular God go back at least two thousand years.

The list goes on and on, and you vacillate between constant crying and utter panic and unchecked rage.

AND THEN (yes, this is me just helping you get all this out, so we're going to have a little protest about everything, we're going to midwife this anger baby), when you dare to bring up any of this, you become a pariah.

*For more information like this that will greatly upset you, please see Beth Allison Barr's excellent book, *The Making of Biblical Womanhood* (Grand Rapids: Brazos Press, 2021).

Why do you always have to be so negative?
Not everyone is like that, you know.
Well, I'm sorry you had such a terrible childhood.
If you hate the church so much, why don't you leave?
Nothing is ever good enough for you.
You're not perfect either.

Yeah. It sucks. It sucks bad, y'all, and unfortunately, we must walk through The Sads. There's a time to really turn over these topics and examine them, but first, not only do we have to grieve, but we also have to go straight up biblical lament.

For those of you who escaped evangelical culture, biblical lament is known for its dramatic calling cards: wearing a sackcloth, rending your garments, and pouring ashes on your head. There is nothing subtle about lament. Think weeping, wailing, gnashing of teeth. Lament is not reserved or proper or within the confines of well-mannered society. Lament grabs you by the shoulders, shakes you violently, and conveys only the agony of loss.

Good thing we've got all these ashes from all that burning-everything-down we did.

But again, I'm bad at The Sads. I needed a little encouragement in exercising my lament muscle, because, well, American Christianity says it's cool with your grief, but I have my doubts, stemming mainly from the complete lack of evidence. So, when I got kicked in the proverbial grief groin one day, instead of being sad, I got confused.

I was standing in the pew of my little church, preparing to receive our weekly blessing from the rector. They always do the announcements before the blessing, so you end up holding your palms out while someone tells you about a men's Bible study at six o'clock on Tuesday mornings or that youth group is canceled this week due to homecoming.

So, this particular week, I was holding out my palms, and an announcement was made about a class that would help us "take our community back for God" or "assist us in our battle against the world." It didn't fully register with me (the back end of these services tends to be wild due to the sheer number of sugared-up kids getting released into the sanctuary, so I had three kids using me as monkey bars), but when the blessing came into my palms, I stood, dumbstruck.

Here we were, organizing classes that would aid in a battle against the world and then getting a blessing: "Go now in peace, to love and serve with singleness of heart." How can I go now in peace to love and serve with singleness of heart when I'm also in a fight against the world? My faith can't call me to hate the world and also attempt to love it. What's peaceful about a battle? (Yes, I know the Scripture about how we shouldn't love the world, but I'm also pretty sure we are supposed to love the people, so if your plan to refute me here was with 1 John 2:15, you can chill the big one.) If I'm at war with everyone who doesn't believe what I believe, how can I possibly open my heart to love them? And what does love even look like, then? I think I actually wiped my palms on my pants, trying, I guess, to remove the weird battle language that seeped in among the blessing.

It just so happened at that moment that the cognitive dissonance of those two concepts hit me right between the eyes. This incident stayed with me for weeks. Why couldn't I shake it? Why was it up my craw like that?

It was about that time I had been seeing a spiritual director for a little bit. I talk to a spiritual director because I do not know how to be contemplative or introspective without someone guiding me through the process. Again, I would rather throw a cream-based casserole at a problem than deal with it, so this is necessary for me.

I explained to my spiritual director what happened, and she nodded in her very calm and discerning way. "Why do you think it has stayed with you?"

I know the point of people like therapists and spiritual directors is to help you reach the answers yourself, but it sure would be great if they skipped all that and just gave them to you.

"It made me sad, and I don't like being sad."

"Say more about that."

And on and on we went. Me, attempting to circumnavigate any complicated spiritual feelings, and her, wishing she'd chosen any other career path, or at least never agreed to take me on as a client.

"Imagine Jesus standing next to you in that pew. What's his reaction?"

This was my least favorite exercise this spiritual director did. And she knew this. One, it feels like casual blasphemy, like I have a Jesus doll and I'm dropping him in with the Barbies to run some fun scenarios like a Ken baptism or Skipper gets saved. Two, how the heck do I know how Jesus would respond to that? But I'd paid her for this, and I'd rather have paid for the potential to figure out why this incident bothers me so much than have paid for another argument about why I hate this exercise, so I closed my eyes and pictured myself standing in the pew, and Jesus next to me.

I don't know how you imagine Jesus (or if you imagine him at all), but my version of Jesus kind of hovers between a lion (thanks, C. S. Lewis), Jonathan Roumie (from *The Chosen*, that one is kind of new), the beatific White Jesus who adorns the weird parlor room hiding in every Baptist church in America, and that composite computer-generated image from *National Geographic* where they decided he looks like the guy selling hot dogs outside the tattoo parlor where you got your first nose ring. So White Lion Hot Dog Jonathan Jesus is standing next to me, and we go through it all over again: my open palms, the kids all over me, we're at war against the world, go now in peace to love and serve with gladness and singleness of heart, through Christ our Lord.

And it's not that White Lion Hot Dog Jonathan Jesus has a reaction to the words or the encounter, but he has a reaction to me, in that he takes my open palms and then looks at me and tells me: *you can grieve this.* And I feel the battle words and the war words seep out of my hands and he says it again: *you can grieve this.* And we just look at each other and my heart feels like it could sink the whole earth to the bottom of the universe.

Now that might sound like bullcorn to you and honestly, I get it. It sounds like a little bit of bullcorn to me. But the moment I said it out loud to my spiritual director, the flood-gates opened, and years of frustration, disgust, anger, hurt, isolation, and plain old fear poured out of my eyeballs like they really had somewhere to be.

What I wanted more than anything was to skip the lament process and move immediately into fix-it mode. I was trying to make all my doubts and questions fit into old wineskins. But I needed to let go of some things. I needed to grieve a system where I could not see how the actions matched the mission statement. I needed to come to terms with how I was complicit in a system that may do more harm than good. I was going to lose people and places and belonging. I was going to uproot my family. I would have to reorient my entire life around this loss. Even the "me" I built was going to have to go.

The permission given to me by White Lion Hot Dog Jonathan Jesus that day was the most important part of my process. It unlocked a key step for me, one I think is easy to miss. While many of us make painstaking efforts to avoid it, grief can be a profound gift. It's the way we signal to ourselves and our people: this means something to me, and I am bereft without it. We're invited to dump the ashes and rend the garments, to pay attention to where we see the disconnect between what is true and what is offered in church, Christianity, Jesus, God, Holy Spirit, ourselves, the whole shebang. Because if we don't, we'll get stuck having the same conversation with ourselves over and over and over and over.

And about those ashes.

They didn't just appear. We torched what we formerly knew, but that doesn't mean everything about our previous experience was worthless or insignificant. Those origins, complicated though they may be, aren't all lamentable. The ashes have purpose. There's a reason you initially called that little plot of land home. There's a reason you started planting and exploring. There's a reason, even if the initial motivation was wonky, that you stayed. Something drew you to this place of faith.

Maybe the value of those ashes for you isn't necessarily a foundational spiritual truth or being compelled by the person of Jesus. Maybe it's the fact that you know how to spot religious abuse now. Maybe it's that your faith is stifled when it attempts to be expressed in traditional, organized ways. Maybe it's that you don't feel the need to find a lesson in every slowly smoldering fire and you inherently understand that lament is enough on its own.

Something else hides in what we might see as superfluous ashes. As a former Boxcar Children reader, I happen to know ash can be used as a cleaning agent and even a disinfectant. We're wounded, and part of this process is cleaning those wounds to get a better idea of what damage we're looking at. It does us no good to ignore them. We will only end up making them worse if we refuse to acknowledge their existence.

And grief doesn't look the same for everyone. When you make space for grief, it takes the form of lament, yes, but also anger at individuals, systems, and maybe even yourself. It can also show up as depression: actual, clinical depression that lays you out in bed for days and makes it hard to fix dinner for anyone.

In that session with my spiritual director that day, she read a James Baldwin quote, one that's stuck with me as I've attempted to navigate a changing and evolving faith. It's offered a good bit of comfort, reminding me that you cannot expect to move forward without mourning: "Any real change implies the breakup of the world as one has always known it, the loss of all that gave one an identity, the end of safety."[2]

The reason change feels hard is because it is. A lot of who I am and who I present myself as to the world is tied up in my very personal faith. And anytime I question my faith, or when my faith is questioned, it feels as though my very being is called into question.* The fabric of who I am becomes wobbly and unstable. When you start the lamenting process, you realize the safety you thought you had when you were building up that little plot of land, before you burned it down, wasn't really safety at all. John Green says, "Grief doesn't change you [. . .] it reveals you,"[3] and it reveals what was holding you up.

That Christmas after Papa died sucked. We tried. We tried so hard. The adults pushed and pulled to bring some semblance of magic into the holiday, but it felt so hollow. By that point, my sweet and precious grandmother, Nene, was

---

*Of course, now I know this is because I had faith simply in myself, and not God. But I didn't get that at the time.

living with my mom and dad, and we all mentally excused her from her traditional duty of pecan pie making, assuming it was off the table, maybe for good. And understandably so. She was so tired. My middle kid, who was still a baby at the time, could get a few smiles out of her, and my eldest would cuddle up at her feet, but she was still locked away in grief.

I don't know when, and I don't know how, but Christmas morning, we woke up to Santa Claus pancakes from my mom and gifts and general revelry because kids make Christmas fun almost no matter what. But on the dessert table, hiding among the pumpkin pie and the apple pie, was a pecan pie baked by my grandmother, an offering to us, a way to say, *Yes, I am sad, but yes, I will keep going.*

The steps we take in grief and lament are crucial to our healing, but no one is saying they are fun. And we can stay there; we can honor that time. We don't have to rush ourselves or hurry the process. We don't have to succumb to, as Professional "Amazingly Miserable" Person Kate Bowler says, "the tyranny of prescriptive joy."[4] And when it is time (and we can trust we will know when it's time) to press onward, to leave the refuge of grief and continue to disentangle our faith, we can approach the process clear-eyed and soul-rested. Maybe our anger still burns. Maybe our hearts still ache. Maybe we've had to completely reorient our lives around this new way of living.

But ash is nature's fertilizer. When it gets in the soil, it detoxifies and readies the land for something new. Ash and all its attendant grief prepare the way for hope, if counterintuitively. Just ask any farmer who's striking their own match—the controlled burn is clearing the way for something good to grow, and that is the hope that remains even as you watch it all burn.

But first, you've got to let yourself feel the loss. So, if we're going to go all in on our lament, where do we begin?

A Baptist Sits Shiva

It's hard to let go anything we love. We live in a world which teaches us to clutch. But when we clutch we're left with a fistful of ashes.

Madeleine L'Engle, *A Ring of Endless Light*

There was not a great amount of Jewish representation in the Texas Panhandle in the 1990s, and I assume that continues to this day. When I was ten, I knew three Methodists and one family of Catholics from the next town over, and my brother and I learned to ride our bikes in the Church of Christ parking lot, but we didn't fraternize because we heard they didn't use instruments and we considered that suspect.

Jews, whether for Jesus or not so much, were an anomaly heretofore unknown.

So when the Jews for Jesus gathered all the Christian churches together at the community center one Sunday night for an all-city worship service, everyone was on high alert. We didn't gather together, ever. The Jews for Jesus did not have the same worship setup we did at FBC Canyon, with our hotly contested drum set that made the older deacons cluck their tongues and shake their heads. A gentleman Jew for Jesus stood outside the community center as everyone entered and blew a horn that looked like he'd walked up to a longhorn steer, wrestled it to the ground, and sawed its rack off. He called it a shofar and I loved it.

The Jews for Jesus read from scrolls in Hebrew! We didn't know any of the words so we just listened, and sometimes they would have us repeat back words like "Adonai" or "Shema," which we dutifully did, but they sounded more like "ADD-DOE-NIGH" and "SHEE-MAW" in our lazy Panhandle mouths. The Jews for Jesus sang songs we did not know! One of them handed Mike Wartes a tambourine, and, other than looking like he wanted to die, Mike did a pretty great job of keeping the beat. The Jews for Jesus danced and clapped! As Baptists, we were not allowed to drink alcohol or dance, but the Methodists looked like they were enjoying themselves, and I was glad for them. The Jews for Jesus wore special worship uniforms, fancy shawls with fringe, and the men even got a tiny hat! (I know now it's a yarmulke or a kippah, but I definitely didn't know that then, so please forgive my youthful error of thinking it was merely a tiny hat.) If there's one thing about ten-year-old girls that's almost universal, it's that they love a fringe moment or a hat moment. The Jews for Jesus brought the big horn out again, and everyone clapped and whooped and hollered. The big horn was a crowd-pleaser, and even the Church of Christ people acted like it was an instrument they could get behind.

That night on the way home, I asked Gwen and Andy* if I could go to the Jews for Jesus church.

"I think I want to be a Jew for Jesus."

*My mother and father, also known by their portmanteau, Gwandy.

"Well, you can't be, really," Mom said, looking at me from the rearview mirror.

"Why not? They believe in Jesus. It's in the name. I liked the big horn. I liked the uniforms. Maybe some of the girls wear the hat sometimes."

"Well, they were just traveling through. And the Jews for Jesus are ethnically Jewish. You are ethnically . . . not."

"What ethnically am I?"

"Caucasian. White. Just White. But you are for Jesus," she said like it was just as exciting. "You're a Baptist for Jesus."

I huffed and crossed my arms. Being a Baptist for Jesus was decidedly not as cool. Our uniforms were itchy tights and shoes I could never find on Sunday mornings. We did not have a big horn.

And so began my lifelong desire to be a part of any faith tradition other than the one I grew up in.

Now I want to be careful because I know we can get into weird fetishizing territory here and I don't want to cross that line. But I do think a mature faith is one that can honor and value what other faith expressions have to offer, and I have learned so much over the years from those outside my tradition. And while I'm certainly no expert, my love and respect for the Jewish faith really helped move me through this first phase of deconstruction, because Jews have a grief tradition that will completely change the way you think about mourning, community care, lament, and how we honor what we've lost.

The word *shiva* literally means "seven," and you might be familiar with the basic idea. When a loved one dies, shiva is the process in which the bereaved move through a cycle of lament in order to be restored. In the case of shiva (or sitting shiva), the idea is to help those who've lost someone walk through their mourning, gently guiding them back into the land of the living.

While we don't have the full meal deal of shiva laid out in the Hebrew Bible, there are examples of pieces of it here and there, as far back as Genesis (or Bereshit, if you're Jewish). You can catch glimpses of shiva in Job, when Job's friends come to sit with him / be mean to him after all the bad things happen. There are the seven-day mourning periods observed by many of the patriarchs, like Joseph and Jacob. But the actual practice wasn't formalized until the thirteenth century, and gosh do I love an ancient ritual with intense metaphorical meaning. I think when we unpack shiva and pay attention to its lessons, we see a powerful way to lament the loss of any part of our faith structure. So let's go.*

The process begins with the most intense period of mourning, known as *aninut*. *Aninut* begins when you hear the news of a loved one's passing and continues up until the burial, and during *aninut* a person is obligated to do . . . nothing of any spiritual consequence. In fact, mourners are exempt from any of the so-called positive commandments like prayer or bestowing blessings or worship. They can plan the funeral, they can sit with the deceased, but *aninut* offers a time of cocooned silence, a way to almost die with your loved one, at least for a little bit.

I think this is such a powerful precept, especially for those of us who spent a long time performing faith. One of the tenets of being evangelical is this phrase that pops up when bad things happen: "And yet, he is good."

Sorry if that just elicited a trauma response for you.

And it's not necessarily that I think that's right or wrong, but it can be used to shut down any real expression of lament.

*I'm very much indebted to Dr. Jen Rosner, who offered wisdom and a watchful eye during the crafting of this chapter. Dr. Rosner's perspectives were crucial to me as I attempted to respectfully offer a window into the observance of shiva as an archetype and avoid appropriation of a faith I respect. I cannot thank her enough.

We can't be mad, we can't be human, we must stomp out every true and honest perception of grief and anguish, faking it in the name of passive evangelism, as if someone will see you lifting your hands in worship while your life is falling apart and want to immediately walk the Roman Road. Because shiva is saying, *Hey, you don't have to do any of that. Here's the permission slip to check out spiritually if you need to.*

I get that makes some of us have a little mini panic attack that we're not lamenting correctly, because maybe you've been conditioned to believe God is not okay with you being a human. I think God knows, and I think it's okay.

So the first gift shiva gives us in our lament process is the acknowledgment that sometimes grief is so great, we can take a break from the outward expressions of religion.

We learned that shiva lasts for seven days, and this part begins right after the burial of your loved one. If someone in your immediate family passes away, you are the one sitting shiva, but if your friend or family member is the one sitting and you're there for support, you simply join the mourner in their home, washing your hands before you enter. Strict observance would include NOT directly comforting the bereaved until postburial. I like to think this is to discourage idiots from offering banal platitudes like "Heaven gained another angel" or "At least she's in a better place" when someone is in shock or pain, which I think should be a universal practice. Or as Sister Anne Lamott so colorfully puts it: "This is the message of the book of Job: any snappy explanation of suffering you can come up with will be horseshit."*[1] So the second gift of shiva is that lament takes time and grief isn't a problem to be fixed or solved but moved through.

*See, this one doesn't count because technically I didn't say it, Sister Anne said it. See how it works?

There's also a little tip in here for your friends and family, so if you want to leave this part open and highlighted or "accidentally" screenshot this and "unintentionally" send it to them, feel free. If you're watching someone you love walk through this lament portion of deconstruction, I know you want to fix it. You want to give them all the right answers and platitudinal Band-Aids because you love them, and you want good things for them. It hurts you to see them not at peace. I get it. I know at some point, my kids will need to go to therapy for the way they were parented, and I understand I will have to swallow this paragraph whole, but the best thing you can do for your person who has set everything on fire with the hope of seeing what's true is to stay with them. Show up. Do not be afraid of their grief, even if you had a hand in it. This might be the hardest thing you've ever done, and it will be so deeply uncomfortable at times you'll wish you could turn yourself inside-out and disappear into your skin. This human (not project or prayer request) is building something, and if you want to be a part of whatever is on the other side, you gotta stick with them.

Back to shiva.

Sometimes a friend will go to your house while you're at the burial of your loved one and cover all the mirrors with a cloth or turn them to face the walls. In ancient Jewish mysticism, there's a belief that when a soul departs from a body, it sort of hangs around our mortal realm for a while. The line between the seen and unseen worlds got a little blurry, and accompanying this hang-out time were possibly some demonic forces that you could not see with the natural eye, but maybe you could see in a mirror's reflection. To be frank, if there's even a 0.001 percent chance I could be going about my business and see a demon in a mirror while I'm plucking a chin hair, I'm off mirrors for life.

As someone with evangelical baggage, but who also starred in a number of Lifehouse skits, I have complicated feelings about actual demons. But, if we look at this through the lens of deconstruction, there can be certain demons that haunt us after the death of someone we love. Regret. Guilt. Remorse. And I appreciate that shiva takes that into account. I also think as we lament whatever it is we're grieving in our spiritual lives post–controlled burn, we're dealing with some of those same demons, and they're important to name. They could be shame, pride, or despair. We're moving through some of the deepest parts of ourselves, so who knows what will surface? This is our chance. Let's not pull any punches while we're here in the lament portion, because I don't know about you, but I have no desire to linger or to come back here any more than we must.

There's more to your bestie coming over to cover up or turn the mirrors around, and shiva considers maybe you're not super feeling the need to put your best foot forward, faking that you're okay. You don't have to carefully apply the makeup, arrange the hair just so, or tidy the clothes, because all your reflective surfaces are out of commission. Shiva says: *No. Not today. Not for these seven days. Relieve yourself of that particular burden.*

I also love that YOU aren't the one covering your mirrors. Someone does it for you, meaning your community supports this. They agree they do not want your fake smile, your Lumify-ed eyes, your anxiety disorder Xanax-ed to hell and back. You do not have to posture for them. Built into shiva is this call to grieve like an actual, proper human without worrying if God is mad at you for having feelings like an actual, proper human. No one is asking you to make it palatable for them. God is certainly not asking that of you.

Another aspect of shiva is seating. Friends will add low stools and remove chairs and couches to allow mourners to sit as close to the floors as possible. Jewish scholars are divided as to whether this practice started as a way to be closer to your loved ones in their burial, to show a lack of personal comfort during a time of mourning, or to show a posture of grief, but the end result is a spirit of humility. Have you ever seen someone forget themselves in grief? It's not something we often witness in Western cultures where we know how to wear a mask well, even in our darkest moments. But in true lament, there is a candor, a frankness, to the point of vulgarity. It's excruciating to watch. Observe the way other cultures grieve and you'll see what I mean. This is not a closed casket funeral, and it will make people uncomfortable. We've removed the buffer between us and the hard things, and now we are left with what remains: the honest truth that something has died.

Can we pause here and just marvel at the stark contrast between the ways we've been taught to grieve and the ways this almost eight-hundred-year-old tradition is encouraging us to lament? We go back to work, we push through, we try to get back to normal as soon as we possibly can. But in shiva, we're invited to take time to sit in it, to get low, to feel it. We don't have to bootstrap and move on after so deep a loss. Our loss deserves our attention and our time.

This practice also shows ways we can be in healthy relationship with our people while we walk through grief. Jews consider a household sitting shiva to be a sacred and holy space, and when someone enters to drop off food or participate in the daily prayers, they might not even knock or ring the doorbell, so as not to disturb the mourners. And when they do get to them, they let the mourners take the lead. They want to talk about how Uncle Geoff loved his rare souvenir spoon collection? Lean in and ask to see it. They want to sit in uncomfortable silence? Go with it. Do they want to rage against the ways Uncle Geoff was a butt and never tipped more than 5 percent? By golly, this is their process, and you let them rage. Giving precedence to the ones who are in the middle of pain allows them to set their own pace, to take this new life at a speed they are comfortable with. When outsiders attempt to control the narrative, not only do they end up stymieing the grief process, but they also leave the mourner unheard and unrecognized. Let those in pain grieve how they need to grieve, and let those who truly love them—so much so they would walk into that house, being mindful to not even knock—ensconce them in a cocoon of safe grace. Shiva says you don't have to have the right answers, you don't have to say the right thing. It also says you can wait to share your real pain with the right people, and we don't have to fill up the space with unnecessary noise when silence will do just fine.

Unlike shiva, the death of a faith that once felt like home is more amorphous, as in there's no body in the living room. But walking through these faith questions, feeling disconnected from your spiritual community, trying to suss out what you believe in isolation, and experiencing anger about the way your faith is expressed in the world—it's a death. It's a death that deserves your lament.

When your faith is used as a political pawn, it's a death.

When the people who carefully placed flannel Jesus on a flannel board post vitriolic memes about immigrants, it's a death.

When churches are known for what they hate and who they exclude, it's a death.

When you scroll through pages and pages of spreadsheets that list sexual abuses covered up by the church leadership, it's a death.

When people who ask good-faith questions are shunned and isolated, it's a death.

I'll tell you what White Lion Hot Dog Jonathan Jesus told me in my imagination: *you can grieve this*. And not only that, but placing arbitrary timelines and guidelines around your grieving process for the sake of propriety or efficiency is cheating yourself out of experiencing God on a level untethered to human parameters. Or as Amanda Held Opelt puts it, "Sometimes we have to allow grief to have its way with us for a while. We need to get lost in the landscape of grief. It is a wild and rugged territory to be sure, but it is here that we meet our truest selves. And we are met by God. The wilderness makes no space for pretense or facade. The language of platitudes and trite niceties are of no use to us in the wilderness. . . . We say what is hard and heartbreaking."[2]

Most people don't ask for death, and most people don't ask to go through deconstruction. There's a whole industry built up around vilifying those in this burning-it-down process, but something rarely said to those walking in it is that you're not "a problem" for seeing the truth. You perceive what most are too afraid or too wrapped up in their own status to acknowledge: something is rotten in Denmark. The puzzle is missing some pieces. You're looking at your Bible and you're looking at the church and you don't see a lot of overlap on that particular Venn diagram. You're looking at the world and you're looking at the character of God and you don't see how God can be real or living or active or good and certainly not all those things at once. You're trying to reconcile Scripture with an understanding of God being love and it's not aligning. And let me tell you: taking that first step of even thinking, *I don't know if I still believe this like I thought I did*, is absolutely terrifying.

You may be afraid, you may be tired, you may be sad, you may be pissed, but you're definitely not the problem.

But, listen, you know how I said my faith upbringing gave me bread and snakes? One of those snakes is the little Religion Cop who lives in my head. He is SUCH a butt, and he's constantly reiterating the old party line, trying to shame me back into the former wineskins. Even writing this chapter, I am wincing, because Religion Cop is sitting up there with his arms crossed, looking very sassy. My face has been in a perma-cringe the entire time because I'm so programmed to just want to rub some dirt in it and move on.

RELIGION COP
All this whining and belly-achin' and complaining about how this person hurt me or how the church did me wrong or whatever isn't doing anyone any good.

I can actually feel some of you thinking that right now as you are reading. But it IS actually doing us good. Because you can't heal what you don't grieve, or, put another way by Fred Rogers, "What's mentionable is manageable."[3] For some of us, our relationship to religion, to church, and to Jesus is what was most dear to us, and the fact that we had to set it on fire ourselves was traumatic enough. That grief we feel is a direct correlation to the love we have for the whole thing. So it's completely normal to grieve and lament a loss of faith community or what your spiritual life looked like. You don't have to pretend that it doesn't wound you.

There are two more parts to the Jewish mourning process. After the seven days of shiva, a mourner will move into *shloshim*, marked by a walk around the block, accompanied by friends. *Shloshim* is thirty days of less intense grief: maybe you go back to work, but no parties, no concerts, no shaving, and no haircuts. You can gradually ease back into society at a pace that works for you. Yes, the chairs get put back and the mirrors get uncovered, but no one has expectations for you to join them at the bar for happy hour. After thirty days of *shloshim*, you move into *shneim asar chodesh*, which is a yearlong mourning. The point is that there is a process to move through that doesn't leave you constantly frustrated or your grief unattended to. There's a process here that helps us let go, to work new muscles around the absence in our world.

When someone dies, we have something of a choice: either let go of unmet expectations—what we thought our lives would look like with them in it, the things we didn't get to say or do—or refuse to acknowledge this is different from what we envisioned. It's the same for our deconstruction process. You don't have to pick right away, but at some point, even not choosing becomes the choice you make. We thought we'd see our kids get married at that church. We thought we'd be surrounded by that community forever. We thought our gifts would be nurtured and celebrated at every stage of life. We thought it would always be the way it was. The harder we grasp on to something that's already gone, the more we end up hurting ourselves, maybe even cheating ourselves out of what could be. Just because one thing is over, just because one thing is the subject of our lament, doesn't mean something else is not growing. Just because you're not getting fed somewhere doesn't mean you have to starve. We've just got to find somewhere else to eat.

Many of us come to this process with certain baggage. There's the baggage we willingly chuck out once we realize we're carrying it, the baggage that's essentially an emotional support animal, and the baggage we've clung to for so long, it's a part of who we are.

True lament takes time, more time than we might think or want. And that's something those of us with an "it's complicated" label affixed to our relationship with Christianity have been conditioned to think we don't have enough of. Who among us does not cringe remembering DC Talk's "I Wish We'd All Been Ready"? "You've been left behind/I hope we'll all be ready." What if we die? What if the rapture happens? But in lament our grief is allowed to work itself out in layers in an incremental process, sometimes doubling back on itself, sometimes taking two steps forward just to take another three back. This is a frustrating truth for anyone who has self-righteously ticked off a checklist to prove their adherence to the process of being (or at least looking) holy. True lament is also not fit for polite society. It doesn't conform to the rules, it doesn't play the game, and it doesn't (to borrow a formerly weaponized phrase) "suffer well."

When I think about this in relation to how we've been taught to "suffer well," I wonder if we might redefine what that means. Maybe it doesn't have to mean suffocating under the weight of unsustainable expectations and performance art. Maybe it looks like addressing questions head-on, even if you're shaking, even if you hate the answers, even if you don't get them. Perhaps it looks like building a new community after losing a treasured one. Maybe your "suffering well" looks like full-throated, honest lament.

Because here's the secret about paying attention to what grieves you and allowing yourself to lament: The way humans become humans to each other is through heartbreak and struggle. No authentic bond can be formed unless two people decide to get vulnerable with each other. Or as Brennan Manning puts it, "One of life's greatest paradoxes is that it's in the crucible of pain and suffering that we become tender."[4] I only know there is more on the other side of this process because someone went first. You only know there is more on the other side because I went before you and there's still a good bit more of this book to go. We need each other, no matter where we might be on our journeys (drink). And the truth is, sometimes during this process, we get cut off from our communities.

I'm going to level with you: there's not an easy answer for that. This can be isolating to the point that you might reconsider the process altogether. I can tell you lots of things like "Be the friend you're looking for" or offer tips like "Volunteer" or "Find your communities online," but your relationships might look a lot different. Your friend group might shift. Your marriage might change. I have some experience with all those aspects, and I can tell you, the loneliness of lament is agonizing at times. The people who were there for you when you toed the line may not be there for you when you set that fire. They may not be comfortable sitting with you in the ash. And it's not a cool feeling. No bow to wrap that up in. It just sucks and I'm sorry.

Lament is also clarifying, which is why I think it's good to start here. That doesn't make it fun, and it might not even make it worth it to you, but it will certainly reveal to you what you're willing to do and where you're willing to go. And you will have to determine if you are willing to remain in uncomfortable relationship with people who, deep in your heart, you know are not willing to go into the tall grass with you. You must be the one who decides if you remain as this version of yourself who isn't really you, but someone built to say "peace, peace" where there is truly no peace. Absolutely no one else can make this choice for you because you are the only one who lives with the consequences. I don't say this lightly at all. No shame, no guilt, but you call the shots.

If you decide to persevere, to push through, however, here's what might happen. What you thought was the end of the world was really something new. Yes, it hurt. Yes, it was awful. Yes, you miss the way things were. But there is still life and hope and goodness on the other side of great loss. When someone we love dies, it feels like we won't ever laugh again. And then one day, we laugh. Joy is not a betrayal; it's our inheritance. Green things will grow again in what looks like a barren place.

And in a couple of years, when you've reached a settled moment, someone will need your perspective. They will need a friend to turn their mirrors around, they will hope there's someone out there who burned it all down and lived to tell the tale, who built something out of the cinders. And there you'll be: matches in hand, not afraid of fields of embers, offering a soft place to land when you never had one.

There's a blessing in lament. And I don't mean that in a trite way because I need to wrap up this chapter. I mean I have receipts. Even with all our currently complicated thoughts and feelings about Jesus and his whole deal, there's an invitation he's extended to us, only available if we give ourselves over to the full weight of what we've lost. "You're blessed when you're at the end of your rope," says The Message paraphrase (Matt. 5:3). "You're blessed when you feel you've lost what is most dear to you" (Matt. 5:4). And not because everyone gets what's coming to them or finally this too shall be made right. "Blessed are the poor in spirit," Jesus says in the Sermon on the Mount, "for theirs is the kingdom of heaven" (Matt. 5:3 NRSV).

It's not that I think if you never go through a deconstruction phase you can't be a true believer. But what I am saying is that, at the very least, this belongs to you just as much as anyone else. This kingdom, God's kingdom, belongs to the bleeding woman who, cast out on the fringes of society, crawled through a crowd in a last-ditch attempt for healing. It belongs to the woman at the well, who questioned and cross-examined and interrogated. It belongs to Thomas, who made Jesus stand there while he stuck his fingers into his side to make, like, *sure* sure. It belongs to Peter, a man whose only consistency was his inconsistency. Heck, it belongs to whichever disciple ran away naked after Jesus got arrested. And it definitely belongs to Jesus himself, who desperately prayed in a garden before his own death for his father to make this stop, please just make this stop.

What lament doesn't do is erase what you had. You don't have to sugarcoat or pretend what you lost was without its flaws. You can be honest about the bread and the snakes, and you can face whatever comes next head-on, not because you're wearing blinders or lying to yourself, but because you've made honest peace with the true nature of what died.

Lamenting what we've lost, what we never had, is a passport stamp into the kingdom of heaven. Jesus said so. Maybe that language makes you uncomfortable, or you have some sort of negative connotation with it, mainly because of all the co-opting. I get it. But I'm talking about the real one. Not the one we've made with lighting design and superficial prayer requests and Sunday morning pleasantries. Not the one we gatekeep to ensure it is pristine and tidy, the kingdom ruled by the false god of power grabs, where hucksters craft elegant sermons creatively sidestepping hard truths so they don't hurt egos or attendance numbers.

When I say the kingdom of heaven is yours, what I mean is: what's true is yours. Fire gets rid of impurities, of fakeness and farce, and leaves only what's real. What's real and true and actual is yours. I mean the kingdom that doesn't screw around. The one with teeth. The one that wails. The one that sweats blood. The kingdom of thick smoke and heavy incense and spit mixed with mud.

Blessed are you crying out in your smoldering field . . .

Blessed are you who sit among the ash . . .

Blessed are you when you find yourself alone with a book of matches . . .

Blessed are you who burned the only safety net you've ever known . . .

For yours is a kingdom where ash isn't just the remnants of what you've burned down.

It's also fertilizer.

It also makes things grow.

ASKING
QUESTIONS

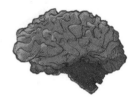

What If the Wrestling Is the Point?

Across two millennia of Christian history—and within
the history of evangelicalism itself—there is ample precedent for sexism, racism, xenophobia, violence, and
imperial designs. But there are also expressions of the
Christian faith—and of evangelical Christianity—that
have disrupted the status quo and challenged systems of
privilege and power.

Kristin Kobes du Mez, *Jesus and John Wayne*

So, you've set your plot of land on fire and maybe you're
panicking a little bit. I get it. It is unmooring at best to look
up from the pile of ashes and your rent garments and realize the thing you've been building all your life is very much
burned to the ground and you are extremely sad and maybe
everyone is talking s-word about you because you're simply
asking a question about the way we're interpreting a certain
verse in Romans chapter one.

It's also unmooring because when your controlled burn
takes out all the trash, you are left with an empty field. And
once you've mourned what was lost to the fire, you might

start to see lots of questions springing up in these open spaces.

If you grew up anything like me, a cute little cucumber pickled in Southern Baptist brine, questions can be considered somewhat dangerous because there was this authoritative aura around doctrine. Everything we believe is The Right Way™ to believe and it's always been this way and everyone else, depending on who they are, is differing degrees of correct and incorrect, some of which will put them at a lower level of heaven, some of which will certainly land them in hell. No one ever came out and said that, but it was understood. The judgment houses at Halloween* really drove the point home.

It's only when you grow up and start looking around a little bit that you discover it's our actual spiritual inheritance to deconstruct and reconstruct.

Scripture is filled with stories of people who had one notion about God, actually encountered God, and then completely changed course.

You do a little digging and learn some of these "ancient doctrines" were made up by someone who drove a 1973 Ford Granada and watched *The Facts of Life*.

All throughout the history of our faith, we see certain time periods where people went: *Hang on. Wait just a damn minute here. We've lost the thread.* And someone or someones of great courage or insanity or both decide to rattle the bones of Christianity and drag everyone by their hair back to the point of this whole thing: Jesus. They stopped majoring in the minors and let the main thing be the main thing, or at least they gave it their best shot.

There are lots of historical and biblical examples of this, depending on your expression of faith or your doctrinal

*That's "JesusWeen" to those in the know.

authority. The Reformation, the Counter-Reformation, Vatican Council II, the Great Schism, the gradual separation of Christianity and Judaism, I could go on. This idea is summed up by one of my favorite thinkers, Phyllis Tickle, who shares the idea by saying how every five hundred years or so, the church undergoes a great rummage sale. And how it's been about five-hundred-ish years since the Reformation, so if the math is mathing, perhaps we're in the middle of one now.

All to say, questions in the life of faith have always been disruptive. This disruption can hurt when it drives a split in the community, a wedge in shared belonging, and differences in vision. This is why, as we've learned, lament is such an important practice. Across the annals of history, disruptions have also presented the invitation to get clear on what is most important.

What are the things we are compelled to make big moves for? For the early Christians, the answer was Jesus. Following him, taking him at his word, living like he asked them to live, and going after God like he did. Living in the kind of freedom he proclaimed. Opening up the gates to include everyone. Big swings for these things.

In a few hundred years, that message would get commercialized by a guy named Constantine, who co-opted the name and person of Jesus for things like killing his enemies in battle and consolidating power, which formed Christianity into a willing and able tool of the Roman empire, which eventually led to Christianity as a dominant power in the Western world.

But at this moment, before Jesus was painted next to a stoic and brave Uncle Sam, at its core, Christianity was about following Jesus. Early Christians (technically on-the-fringe Jews and their weird Gentile friends) met in houses. They fed single moms and housed the unemployed. They pooled resources without worrying about a 401(k). They tended the sick (and sometimes they straight-up healed them) and they did their best to make sure everyone had what they needed. They were messy as all get-out. People still peopled. But at the end of the day, they leaned on the precious words of Jesus, handed down from those who heard him say them. Those are the roots from which Christianity grew. That is our spiritual inheritance. It is buried somewhere underneath fussing over who can lead who in what and prayer in school and banning drag brunch and being afraid of critical race theory. We can find it again.

Then if you want to get real weird, you might consider that one of the greatest eras of deconstruction comes from our guy Jesus himself. First, let's look at the Jewish concept of messianism. Throughout the books of the Prophets in the Old Testament, we see hints of the idea of the Messiah. To modern Christian eyes and ears, we've been trained see Jesus around every corner of the Old Testament, like a *Where's Waldo* book. He's popping up in the prophecies, and any time someone mentions a messiah,* we're like, *that's our guy, we call it, no takebacks.*

The language around the Messiah was also important. Liberation was a huge component of Messiah talk. He will set you free. He will break your chains. He will release you from bondage. So naturally, an oppressed people group like the Jews at this time, who were abused by the Roman Empire, saw this liberation as political. *When the Messiah comes, we will be free from Rome. He will break the Roman chains. He*

---

*Again, I know this is simplifying the Jewish concept of messianism; there were actually multiple messiahs and all sorts of different prophecies for messiahs! It's really complicated and way more nuanced than I can easily explain here, but I must mention this or people with real seminary degrees will write ugly one-star reviews on Goodreads. They may still do that, but at least not about this. Please do not consider this a personal challenge.

will release us from Roman bondage. This was the narrative. What else could it be?

The vision was hot, conquering hero. The mood board was Hercules, a Jewish hero like Samson without the complicated lady situationship. Maybe someone born into a house of the priesthood, someone with a lot of clout and power in these difficult times. The Messiah would need connections and influence to get the job done. He would need money to build an army if they were going to eradicate the most powerful political force in the world. The people knew exactly how it would go and what it would look like.

Of course, in retrospect, if you believe Jesus was the Messiah, we know that's not how it went. Instead of power, we got a backwoods, nobody carpenter. Instead of being born into the priesthood, we got someone born into scandal. Instead of money, we got a guy who had to rely on rich ladies to fund his ministry. No army. No connections. Just a guy and disorganized dudes and random ladies on the fringes of society. Not all that impressive.

But the most important "instead of": Instead of liberating the people from Roman taxes and authority, this Messiah wanted to liberate their souls. Instead of changing Roman hearts about conquering them, this Messiah wanted to give his people a new heart: one of flesh to replace their heart of stone. He was doing something completely different from what they thought he was here to do.

Most rabbis and scribes considered their interpretation of the Scriptures, of a conquering political hero, to be accurate. But with his arrival, Jesus deconstructed the historical interpretation and reconstructed it to help his people better understand its original purpose.

And hot damn! This made people mad, for a few reasons. One, they really hated the Romans and wanted out from under their thumb, and two, no one likes to be wrong, especially people who are professionally supposed to be right. And frankly, sometimes it pisses us off that we don't get tangible relief. No sense in not looking that right in the eye. We'll get to it.

This was part of the deconstruction/reconstruction journey (drink) of Jesus. He wasn't about individual shaming but used his experiences with individuals to draw attention to the ways God's Word and God's ways were being perverted and manipulated to serve power. I mean, look at this smoke from Matthew: "Don't set people up as experts over your life, letting them tell you what to do. Save that authority for God; let *him* tell you what to do. . . . There is only one Life-Leader for you and them—Christ" (23:9–10). And then he just absolutely lights up religious leaders who work to keep people out of God's kingdom. It's a good read, highly recommend.

Let's take Jesus's encounter with the woman at the well, or Photine, as she's known traditionally (shout-out to whoever went back and named all the unnamed women in the Bible). Photine was a Samaritan, a woman who'd had five husbands, a woman who was very much in her *Reputation* era. All of this made her a prime candidate for being a social pariah, which is why she was at the well alone that day when Jesus popped up. Nice Jewish men did not speak to women they weren't related to, and definitely not alone. They certainly didn't speak to Samaritan women (Samaritans and Jews were the biggest rivalry in town), and they'd eat a shrimp before they consorted with a woman who had a shady past.

But Jesus, who had wandered away from his handlers (Don't you know he did this all the time?), doesn't seem worried about any of that. He shows Photine how her people and his people had strayed from knowing who they really

were, and he offers her living water. It's not about where
you're worshiping or who's right or who's more powerful.
He wants her to know the way she's living, the way she's
operating, even the way she's worshiping, it doesn't have to
be like this. She can walk in freedom. Life can look different.
The truth was even better than she could have ever imagined.
But I love that she isn't just like, "Wow, sounds amazing,
thumbs up, everything is great now." Sister Photine lawyers
up. She's got questions and even when she realizes who Jesus
is, she's not one bit embarrassed or ashamed that she asked
them. Nor does Jesus chastise her for asking them. In fact,
they were how she got to the truth in the first place.

Or what about the Sermon on the Mount? We've talked
about Jesus blessing these people, and, by default, us in our
lament, but can you imagine the confusion on the faces of
the people as Jesus cried out, "If you even think about being
mad at your brother, you might as well have gone and mur-
dered him!" These people are all prepped for a light sermon
followed by dinner on the fellowship hill, and he comes out
with, "If you want to be pure, the second you start lust-
ing, just pluck your eye out!" Or "If you divorce your wife,
you're responsible for making her an adulteress! Just FYI,
everyone!"

He started out all these fun little tidbits with the phrase
"You've heard it said . . ."

"You've heard it said that, but now I'm saying this."

"You thought this was the case, but now I'm telling you
this is the case."

This is how the New International Version puts it:

You have heard that it was said to the people long ago, "You
shall not murder, and anyone who murders will be subject
to judgment." But I tell you that anyone who is angry with

a brother or sister will be subject to judgment. . . . You have heard that it was said, "You shall not commit adultery." But I tell you that anyone who looks at a woman lustfully has already committed adultery with her in his heart. . . . You have heard that it was said, "Eye for eye, and tooth for tooth." But I tell you, do not resist an evil person. If anyone slaps you on the right cheek, turn to them the other cheek also. . . . You have heard that it was said, "Love your neighbor, and hate your enemy." But I tell you, love your enemies and pray for those who persecute you." (Matt. 5:21–22, 27–28, 38–39, 43–44)

There needed to be a reframing. A reset. A deconstruction (if you will) of what the people thought this thing was about, followed by a reconstruction (if you will) of what Jesus knew this thing was about.

Jesus was not only calling his people to live to a higher standard but also underlining all the ways we could never perfectly follow the law of Moses. We could never sacrifice enough, we could never have enough burnt offerings. There was only one way to life abundant. There was only one way to a heart of flesh. They were going to have to fully trust him. They were going to have to believe he was who he said he was. They were going to have to take God seriously.

Even Jesus's death flipped the script on the expectations people had for him. He was the Messiah; he wasn't supposed to die. And he certainly wasn't supposed to die before he fulfilled his purpose. Instead of whipping the Romans into submission, they whipped Jesus. Instead of bringing them under his authority, they humiliated and killed him.

Look all throughout the Gospels and you'll find a Jesus subverting every prophetic expectation placed on him at every turn. A Jesus deconstructing all the projections his people placed on him for generations.

I'm really drilling down on this because I know that for some of you, the person of Jesus is part of the reason you set your controlled burn to begin with. Maybe you struggle with the historical Jesus, or you view Christianity as colonized Judaism, or you think Jesus was a great teacher, but not the Son of God. I've considered all those options as well, so I know where you're coming from. And my goal is not really to convince you otherwise (plenty of books already around on that), but just to show you maybe he deserves a second look. No figure in American culture is more hijacked than Jesus, and it's pretty easy to make him mascot of whatever cause you need him to stand for. So, if you're unfamiliar with him or it's been a while, you might be tempted to think he wears an American flag as a sash or that he only shows up in the key change or even that he's White Lion Hot Dog Jonathan Jesus. A lot of us were introduced to a Jesus invoked in "thoughts and prayers" but no concrete actions. A Jesus who sneered at welfare and food stamps but looked the other way for a church tax exemption. A Jesus with his legs cut out from under him twice: once on the cross, and then once more by the church.

But I think it's key to recognize that at the heart of this faith we're working through right now, there's a guy who is taking what we thought we knew and flipping all of it on its head. And I don't mean that in a cute way. I mean it in a radical and comprehensive way. I mean that when his mother was pregnant with him, she sang a song with such powerful themes of liberation and justice, the British Empire banned that section of Scripture during its colonization of India for fear it would cause an uprising. I mean that a simple touch of his hand would resurrect dead cells and reanimate lifeless limbs. Women boldly wasted their futures by destroying the one thing of value they owned, using it to anoint his feet instead of for a dowry. Somehow the atoms he himself arranged that made up fish and loaves of bread multiplied into more atoms that made up fish and loaves of bread, so much more there was an abundance. Water was so enamored it forgot to keep its physical properties and could not help but hold him up. Jesus set up shop here for a moment to shake the dust out of what we thought we understood about God and who God is and who we are. How we are free, who makes us so, and what our freedom compels us to do. What love is, why we love, and where that love enables us to go.

This is not a man afraid of a question.

Until we make peace with the fact that the guy we claim to follow is not only okay with this, but he started the whole shebang, we're never going to feel we have permission to ask our questions with our whole chest. Just like lament, we shouldn't half-ass the questioning portion of our process. If we don't put our foot in it, we'll be right back where we started.

But Religion Cop is alive and well in your head. It's possible you've been programmed to believe that asking questions is not okay. Or that you just need to have faith. Or that it's been this way for thousands of years, so suck it up, buttercup.

But we've actually been doing the questioning thing for thousands of years, individually and corporately. You need to know that this whole process is not new. It feels scary, it feels isolating, and it feels overwhelming. You might even get some pushback. But even if you're reading this as a member of an older generation and thinking, *Well I never went through all of this*, you probably did. You might not have given it a name or posted about it on Instagram or burned it all down, but you almost certainly adjusted or had to untangle a belief you grew up with after encountering God in a new way, because it's built into the DNA of our faith to constantly reevaluate, to recalibrate, to rethink, to renew, to reconsider. That's what an active faith does.

The history of Christianity could probably be blamed for most of the world's problems today. I will be the first to say Christians have perpetuated* some of the worst crimes against humanity ever, and I have no doubts we will corporately continue in this pattern, much to my great dismay.

I also know we've besmirched doubts, questions, and exploration to the point that, when you finally admit that you are disenchanted, disconnected, and at odds with what you once believed, you start feeling a little unhinged.

In fact, looking again at our heritage of faith, when you examine the great mothers and fathers who made an impact, it's like . . . wait.

Are we supposed to struggle with this?

Is this part of the whole package?

Is this a feature, instead of a bug?

Let's look at the evidence, starting with Mother Teresa. We can pretty much all agree Mother Teresa is universally seen as an icon of the Christian faith. She gave up her life to serve the dying poor of India, she had some banger one-liners ("If you judge people, you have no time to love them"), and she met Princess Di. All solid high points. Seems like Mother had it figured out. And yet! Here's what she wrote to one of her spiritual confidants: "There is so much deep contradiction in my soul. Such deep longing for God—so deep that it is painful, a suffering continual—and yet not wanted by God. Repulsed, empty, no faith, no love, no zeal.

*And are perpetuating!

105

Souls hold no attraction. Heaven means nothing. To me, it looks like an empty place—the thought of it means nothing to me, and yet this torturing longing for God. Pray for me please that I keep smiling at Him in spite of everything."[1]

What about Martin Luther King Jr.? A minister of the gospel, the face and hands and feet of the Civil Rights Movement in the United States during the 1960s? He admitted himself that although he called himself a Christian his whole life, "It was kind of an inherited religion, and I had never felt an experience with God in the way that you must . . . if you're going to walk the lonely paths of this life."[2]

And what about the other Martin Luther? Staunch defender of the faith (depending on who you're talking to, I suppose) who once went toe-to-toe with His Holiness, the pope? Who also wanted to give up on life and described his depression by saying, "I am but a ripe stool, and the world a giant asshole. Soon we shall but part."[3]

Or one of my favorite spiritual thinkers, Henri Nouwen, a Catholic priest who spent the last part of his life serving adults with mental disabilities in France. He wrote: "For most of my life I have struggled to find God, to know God, to love God. I have tried hard to follow the guidelines of the spiritual life—pray always, work for others, read the Scriptures—and to avoid the many temptations to dissipate myself. I have failed many times but always tried again, even when I was close to despair."[4]

Does everyone wrestle so hard like this? Surely the Bible will have some folks who felt more at ease in a life of faith.

Oh, my sweet summer child. Let's talk about perhaps the best-known wrestler of the faith. Jacob.

What Scripture wants you to know about Jacob right off the bat is that he's a trickster and has been from the jump. He's trying to hoodwink the midwives into thinking he's the firstborn at his birth. He's working behind the scenes with his mom to defraud his twin, Esau, out of his birthright blessing, a huge deal in ancient Mesopotamia (imagine your little brother tricking your parents into giving him all your inheritance and his after they won the lottery), forcing him to flee. And while you thought you couldn't play a player, Jacob is also getting double-crossed by his future father-in-law into marrying the not-as-cute daughter before he can marry the cute daughter, which definitely did not have far-reaching consequences, why do you ask?

So now it's time for Jacob, his cute wife, his not-as-cute wife (which I have thoughts about but there's no time!), and all the sons and daughters he's accumulated over the years to return to the land of his father, which means he's also returning to the land of his brother. You know, the one he kind of stole everything from. The one whom he hasn't seen since he tricked him out of his birthright. The one who is probably still pretty pissed.

Jacob's a lot of things, but an idiot is generally not one of them. So he makes some strategic decisions: he sends Esau some gifts to soften him up, he divides his camps, and he starts praying like he has a test in five minutes he forgot to study for. Sleep evades him, so he takes a walk, running smack dab into . . . well, that's actually a great question.

The identity of this entity has been debated since we found this particular scroll. Is it just a guy? Is it Jacob's conscience? Is it Michael the archangel? Is it a malevolent river-demon? Later in the story, Jacob straight up says it's God but he also says it's an angel. Is it the angel of the Lord?

Funny thing about the angel of the Lord in the Hebrew Bible. Sometimes when we read about the angel of the Lord, it indicates an actual angel (not a fat cherub cutely staring off into the distance or a buff, hot blond dude in a robe, we're

talking wheels of fire with eyes). But some Christian scholars believe in a few of these instances, the angel of the Lord
designates something called a Christophany, an appearance
of the preincarnate Christ outside of the normal places we
might find him (like the Gospels, where he is a human Jesus).

And naturally, the angel of the Lord (whoever or whatever
that is) and Jacob wrestle, as one does.

Have you ever heard of anything that aligns so perfectly
with eighth-grade boy energy?

School bus after a long day of education?

We should wrestle.

Home watching a movie and someone gets bored?

We wrasslin'.

Meet a supernatural stranger in a dark desert the night before you're supposed to reunite with your estranged brother?

Do you smell what the Rock is cooking?

We don't know what time WWE began for Jacob and the
angel of the Lord, but Scripture says they wrestled all night.
Can we get more information? Does a fifth-century monk
not want to slip a little commentary in there? Did Jacob and
the angel have any kind of conversation? Did either of them
comment on how weird this was? Did they have an audience,
like a Eurasian coot or a couple of other angels who wanted
a closer look? What was the point of it?

Because I am a Bible nerd and I have been taught by Dr.
Wilda Gafney to hone my sanctified imagination when I read
Scripture, I often ponder Jacob's inner thought life during
this wrestling match. What did he fear? What were his re-
grets? What did he hope would come from all of this? We
don't know and can only speculate, but Jacob was a human,
just like us, and if it were me, I'd be up in my feelings about
some of those things. I'd be a little desperate. I'd be looking
for any way to get an edge to protect myself and my family,

to try and make things right with my brother. Barbara Brown Taylor says it this way: "Who would stick around to wrestle a dark angel all night long if there were any chance of escape? The only answer I can think of is this: someone in deep need of blessing; someone willing to limp forever for the blessing that follows the wound."[5]

The sun rises and the writer of Genesis says the angel of the Lord wins with a move he could've used all night long and didn't: he touches Jacob's hip, throwing it out of socket and disabling his opponent.

And even then, Jacob won't let go.

The angel of the Lord is like, "My guy, the sun is up. We're done here. Let me go."

Jacob shakes his head. "I'm not letting you go until you bless me."

It's not in the text, but I do picture the angel of the Lord laughing here. "Alright, what's your name?"

"Jacob."

"Not anymore. From now on, we're calling you Israel. You've wrestled with God and come out the other side."

And then Jacob names the spot Peniel. Which Sunday school teachers will mispronounce for generations, causing immature eighth-grade boys to start slapping and hitting each other all over again.

What a bizarre story. And how much more absurd to think this is the story we are invited into—not one of checklist certainty, but one in which God says openly, "Let's have it out."

When my brother and I were little, when it was just the Core Four, we used to wrestle with my dad during the commercial breaks of whatever TV show we were watching that night. *The Cosby Show, Home Improvement, Star Search*, whatever it was, Dad would always pull us off the couch by our feet, Drew and I screaming in fake protest, my mother scrunching up her face at the sheer volume of the TV, the squealing children, and her husband pretending to be Hulk Hogan (boy, do I understand this face now that I too wonder as a mother how people can be so loud and so unaware). There wasn't really a goal to these wrestling sessions: they probably served to wear us out before bedtime, but the idea was to be on top. If you were at the bottom, you were getting squished. The only rule was that when the commercials were over, everyone yelled, "Show's back on, show's back on!" and you had to stop wherever you were in the pile.

It usually ended up with my little brother on Dad's back, Dad acting like my sixty-pound brother was too heavy for him to be able to return to his chair, and little old me, smushed at the bottom. My strategy was always to dramatically gasp, "I can't breathe! I can't breathe!" until my mom finally had enough and gave Dad the stink eye and a perfectly intoned "Andy" and shut it down. But after every commercial break, we would disentangle ourselves from the pile of arms and legs and elbows and knees and go back to snuggling with Mom, only to once again be pulled off the couch during the next ad for Mr. Bucket.

This went on until one day I guess I got too cool for commercial break wrestling. My brother and Dad kept it up for a while, but I think they missed the theatrical work I brought to the table, and it just kind of petered out. I'm sure my mother was thrilled to finally be able to hear a commercial for the first time in probably ten years.

And then I had kids, and watching my parents become a Yaya and a DoDad is wonderful if not strange. These are not the people who washed my mouth out with soap for simply asking if "ass" was a bad word.*

As my kids have gotten older, Dad pulled out something called The Claw. My brother and I never got The Claw as kids that I recall, but The Claw is a lot like commercial break wrestling. Leading up to a visit, when we FaceTime with Yaya and DoDad, one of the kids will ask if DoDad is bringing The Claw. He says he's not sure. Do we need it? Someone will mention that a sibling definitely needs The Claw. When they get to our house, someone will taunt my father, "Sounds like I need The Claw." And off they go.

We've never really said this out loud, but The Claw is part of my kids' heritage in a way. I don't think I've ever explicitly told them about commercial break wrestling, but it's just something our family does with each other.

I'm not suggesting that Jacob and Maybe Secret Old Testament Jesus were having commercial break wrestling or giving each other The Claw. My point is there's a throughline here of "this is what we do in this family." We tussle. We work it out. We get messy. Our spiritual family is no different. Jacob kicked it off for us: having it out with God is embedded in the DNA strands of our souls.

Grappling with the God of the universe, if you're ready to do that, takes balls (you have to be tender), and it takes a uterus (you have to be tough). What the story of Jacob reveals to us about our spiritual inheritance is that God is ready, willing, and able to scrap in the dark desert over all the things that piss us off, the stuff that wounds us, the injustices in the world, and why God made all this so damn hard sometimes. God can take it. And it's not even that God

*I'm sorry for how many times I've said "ass" in this book, Mom. The soap didn't take.

is tolerating us, rolling those giant God-eyes in annoyance while we're having it out. Go back to that weird hip touch the angel of the Lord puts on Jacob as the sun rises. The angel could have made that move at any point during the night and the thing would have been over. And whether this is a physical fight or some sort of spiritual metaphor, the fact remains that this supernatural being, sent by God or maybe some version of God, doesn't brush Jacob off with a glib answer or a Hobby Lobby cliché. Jacob is met with a force equal to his own, a dueling partner who respects his struggle enough to honor him with a real match. Jacob gets a new name. Jacob gets blessed.

And it's not just Jacob. It's also Job, who came full force at God. Photine, who, to be fair, didn't know she was talking to God, but she got in his chili. Hagar, who cried out to God for some reprieve, for crying out loud. Abraham, who either gave God the silent treatment after the incident with Isaac and the ram or had a discussion so volatile it was kept off the books. Nicodemus, who cornered Jesus into an all-night theological symposium. The Syrophoenician woman, who arm-wrestled Jesus so hard that, if we believe the text (and I think we should), she forced him to reconsider his perspective and got a healing out of it. As Ben Moon says, "I can beat on God's chest. I think it's big enough."[*] Get in there. Have it out.

Wrestling is also . . . so weird. Yes, it's intimate. Yes, it's personal. And the face-to-face wrestling is how we get close, no doubt. But it's also awkward. Have you seen real wrestling, WWE wrestling, any of it? So much skin slapping. So much embarrassing eye contact. You can't hide anything.

[*]Benjamin R. Moon, *Wise Words I Say In Between Maintaining My Duolingo Streak* (Kitchen Table Talks, since 1983).

112

The clothes are too tight. The tricks are too obvious. You feel a little silly, exposed, like you don't know where to put your hands or where to grab onto. It's just you and the other person, grappling and tussling and just so in each other's space.

And maybe your beef isn't actually with God or Jesus; maybe it's more with Scripture or Christian nationalism or the church or something like that. Mount up. The answer you were given to a question you asked when you were ten (or ten months ago) may not be the only way that question has been answered historically. In fact, there may be dozens of ways that question has been answered by faithful scholars across history.

Speaking of scholars, they have a hard time saying definitively what the etymology of the word *Israel*—Jacob's new name—is. We definitely know the back part, "El," means God, but the front part is a little murkier. *Strive, fought, contended, wrestled*: all these words make the cut. So, when the angel of the Lord renamed Jacob, the angel didn't change his name to "He who is blessed" or "He who did something bad to his brother a long time ago." Jacob's name changed to "He who wrestles." Amy-Jill Levine broke this open for me in her book *The Difficult Sayings of Jesus* when she connects that point to the descendants of Jacob. The name *Israel* was conferred on all Jacob's descendants. The people of Israel are the people who wrestle with God. The people who fight with God. The people who strive with God.

Levine carries that honorific as a Jew, and when Jesus flung open the windows and kicked down the door for us Gentiles to come to the party, I believe I was adopted into that as well. When Jesus offered up a new covenant, one fixed in the reality of his death and undomesticated hope of his resurrection, anyone who claims a branch of that family tree is a part of that spiritual heritage: grappling with the

Creator of the universe, tussling with God, refusing to let go of Divine Love.

If the believer/Christian/follower of Jesus identity feels iffy, complicated, or conditional to you, maybe this vision strikes truer. We joyfully affirm nothing less than this: we are the people who have it out with God. Not the people who have it all figured out, not the blindly obedient, not the quietly acquiescent, not the easily answerable, not the willingly paid off. And what's more, we are people who can trust that God is not threatened, offended, or angered by this, but to the contrary, God is honored. I think God's into it.

Scripture does not venerate the stories of people who obeyed God before they saw God could be trusted. We all know our deepest relationships and strongest bonds are with those who have the guts to say hard things, who call us out, who choose to stay amid persistent questions and skeptical button pushing and even when we're not our best selves.

If you've been the bearer of doubts, it's possible a well-meaning (or less-than-well-meaning) person has suggested that you strengthen your faith. A strong faith in today's vernacular is identified as one that does not ask questions. If we just don't look our misgivings in the eye, repeat Scripture until it's meaningless, and grit our teeth to push through our own cognitive dissonance about all the ways we want to just give up, everything will be fine, thank you so very much. But this is faith that just has faith in itself, predicated on nothing at all, a house of cards. You can shadowbox all day, but it doesn't build muscle like fighting with an actual opponent. Lobotomizing the part of yourself that is angry, hurt, or frustrated with God is not the answer.

Beloved, you have a strong faith because you wrestle, not in spite of your wrestling. It is a gift. Don't believe anything to the contrary.

We were not called to be certain about anything. We were not called to put our trust in our interpretation of Scripture or easy answers or the state of the world or other believers or the institution of church or leaders.

God has told Jacob to return to the land of his father, because God wants to bless him there. Not one part of the process turns out to be easy or uncomplicated, and now a new wrench in the plan: what he assumes is his still-furious, bitter brother headed toward him, ready to exact the vengeance he's longed for all this time. So, Jacob prays and wrestles, and finally the angel of the Lord gives him a little underhook hip toss because Jacob simply will not relent. He is so scared of what is coming. His future is so uncertain. He thought he could trust God; didn't God say they wanted Jacob to come back? Didn't God say they wanted to bless Jacob? And now God just brought Jacob all this way so that Esau could murder him? The angel of the Lord has to put him out of commission to ask Jacob: *Will you give me a shot? I'm not going to abandon you. I brought you here for a reason. If you give me a chance, I'll show you how I can love you. Will you trust me?*

The text does not say the angel of the Lord hurts Jacob. It says he limps, but it does not say there is pain. I think this is an important thing to recognize. Jacob has a reminder of his wrestling match, but it's not torture or God teaching Jacob some sort of vindictive, look-what-you-did-you-little-jerk lesson. It's that he walks a little differently. He carries the reminder with him, an Ebenezer embedded in his very bones.

This untangling, this deconstruction, this demolition, this offering of trust and our hope and hesitation over whether we should take it: this is the work of our lives. There's no finish line, no final destination, no arrival platform with flowers and posters of welcome. You don't reach an end phase of faith and beat the Big Boss and save the princess. It's not a game you can win. You're a person in a relationship. It will take time. It is there and available. It will take patience. You can be gentle with yourself. It will make you tired. You can rest! But it's a process that wants nothing more than for you to bring your whole self into the ring. And a question hangs in the air: *Will you trust me?*

When you feel off-kilter, when you're alone in your curiosities, when you feel judgmental stares, when you feel torn apart by unanswerable questions, remember:

Having it out with God is your spiritual heritage. The wrestling is not the problem, it is the point.

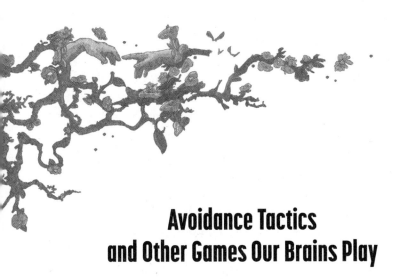

Avoidance Tactics
and Other Games Our Brains Play

You don't think your way into a new kind of living. You
live your way into a new kind of thinking.

Henri Nouwen, *Life of the Beloved*

For an entire religion premised on having it out with God,
it's wild when you consider how normalized it has become
in the Christian tradition to ignore and suppress all the parts
of you that question anything.

Do you have doubts? No, you don't.

Are you curious about something and maybe it's caused
you to wonder if an "established fact" is a little wobblier than
you thought? That is evil, unfortunately. Please back away,
lest you inadvertently sign up for a slot in hell.

Has Holy Spirit been stirring in you a question that was
asked and definitively answered long ago? You'd do good
to shape up and follow correct teachings. Your heart is
deceitful. Your mind is evil. Concepts like skepticism and

curiosity get replaced with cautionary tales of backsliding. And even if you end up in a spiritual community that is okay with doubts or questions or struggles, we still have not fully figured out how to honor those without the awkward attempt to paper over them as quickly and quietly as possible. So, what I'm saying is, when you finally come to terms with the fact that you actually have questions, it might take you a minute to voice them. And when you voice them, they might not get the reception you were hoping for.

A Hard Truth I Have Learned: Humans will do just about anything to avoid disruption because disruption does not feel safe. And the reason it does not feel safe is because our brain is telling us it is not safe. Which is not technically true. Your brain is really just not interested in changing its mind about anything. Call it efficient, call it lazy, but it's very content to keep firing those synapses in the settled grooves it has been creating over time. Sleeping on a particular side of the bed, your coffee routine, and the belief systems you've upheld your entire life. The work of creating new neural pathways? No thanks, we're good.

Dr. Ralph Lewis defines the way our brains use belief to understand and navigate our world: "[Beliefs] are the mental representations of the ways our brains expect things in our environment to behave, and how things should be related to each other—the patterns our brain expects the world to conform to."[1] But once our beliefs are set, once we lock in those expectations, it becomes monumentally difficult to change them, or even to consider changing them.

There's a concept in psychology called belief perseverance, where to keep our brains from short circuiting, people will cling to their "cherished notions." This means that when you're met with something that doesn't fit within your established working theory of the world, you'll either dismiss it or just think of it as a random exception. So, when presented with new information, you tend to resist, because disruption equals not safe.

Our brains will even go so far as to change our memories to better fit with our beliefs. Dr. Nan Wise points out that "our minds are largely habit-making machines. We often stick to the habitual way of doing things,"[2] and we'll just keep doing that until what we're doing stops working for us. And some of us will still keep doing it, even past that point. Not only that, but changing our mind raises our cortisol levels, which stresses us out physically. As in things like panic attacks and heart attacks. You know, a thing that makes you feel like you're dying and a thing that could actually kill you.

So it's no wonder everyone loses their mind when we challenge any previously held understanding. Our brains are very busy reminding us about the dentist appointment tomorrow, remembering all the dumb things we probably said in that one social interaction, and still perfectly recalling all the lyrics to every Nelly song from the early 2000s. It doesn't particularly like expending energy when it doesn't have to, i.e., ruminating on religious nuances that were thought to be done and dusted a long time ago. It also thinks we might be dying. The brain is tired, so when it can, it shortcuts belief.[3]

We all do this, right? We follow people on social media who believe like we do, we play around in our little confirmation bias echo chambers. Our faith spaces tend to bolster our beliefs instead of challenge them. We read books and listen to podcasts and support people who are "vetted" as part of the group in one way or another. And that's not bad. There's nothing wrong with living in community with people who believe similarly to you, who encourage you.

But something happened every single time you've acted on a belief or experienced something that affirmed a conviction. The little workers in your beautiful brain got out their shovels and trucks and went to work, digging a groove even deeper to remember that particular pathway, to smooth the road down to make the next trip even easier. So, for example, if all you've heard your entire life is that the Bible is the inerrant word of God, there's a shortcut in your brain to reach that conclusion. We hear it, it's already programmed in, and we don't have to reprocess the statement each time it's presented to us. What's more, anytime we are confronted with something to the contrary, we almost immediately reject it, not because we're necessarily bad people or we're not curious, but because our brain is already halfway down the shortcut by the time we've thought to challenge the question.

When we establish a belief as a still-developing human (remember, our brains are essentially cake batter until we turn twenty-five years old, according to Instagram psychology),[4] not only are the brain shovels sharper and the cognitive trucks newer, but it's much easier to dig into cake batter than it is to smash stones or lay asphalt. That's why little kids can be fluent in a second language by the time it takes a grown adult with a mortgage to learn how to properly say *por favor* with the rolling of the *r*'s and everything. This is why developmental PTSD is much more difficult to navigate, because the grooves were cut in cake batter, and then they hardened into stone.

BUT THEN.

A disruption occurs. It could be a death. The loss of a job or position. Maybe it was a global tragedy or a reordering of the political landscape. Maybe there was an upheaval in the way you saw or understood another person. But whether it's a lived experience or just a different way of looking at things, you're presented with something new to consider.

Before we ever unleash the beast on anyone else, we must convince our own brains a change, any change, is worth fighting for. The call is coming from inside the house. When you try to change a belief, you are met with your own resistance. When we need to reexamine something we believe, we attempt to move from primitive brain functions to more complex ones, which is exhausting, both mentally and physically. Your brain tries to double down on whatever you believed before because it's just easier. Or again, maybe you might be dying. You keep it to yourself, you roll it around in your brain, you might crack open your Bible or search for a podcast to listen to on the subject. But it automatically feels wrong. Or defeating. Or pointless. Or debilitating.

On the other hand, there's this little plot of land you burned to the ground that seems to need some attention. Requiring active participation. Some give-a-damn. And honestly, maybe that sounds exhausting.

That's not to say that disruption always brings change to our belief systems. I think there are times when our beliefs anchor us during seasons of disruption and change, and not every major life event is meant to bear the good fruit of meaningful modification. Disruption can also be a time to firmly plant us in the bona fides, as opposed to undoing some of those mala fides.

But how on earth do we tell the difference? For our spiritual ancestors like Jacob, we get the benefit of hindsight. Wait for an angel of the Lord or a burning bush or a prophetess. But for us, caught up in the pesky fact of living in the present, we often find ourselves searching for signs, phoning a friend, or dusting off an old evangelical word thrown around liberally but seldom understood (at least by me): *discernment*.

Of course, there's regular discernment, which is just asking, Are you an idiot or not? Can you make good choices? It's often linked with a perceptiveness, a wisdom, a sensitivity. And in the biblical sense, discernment can overlap with some of that. But spiritually, discernment is one of those smooshy areas (that's the scientific term). What's sagacious for one is errant for another, and the width and breadth of our faith is vast enough that we've been splitting up over who has it right and who has it wrong since the whole thing started, to speak nothing of our personal lives.

It's smooshy because there's a lot that swirls together to make up discernment. Holy Spirit, your own brain, your lived experiences (and by default, the experiences you have not lived), the people around you (and by default, the people not around you), how you interpret Scriptures (and you guessed it, how you don't), and the list goes on. But if we're going to get serious about the process of asking questions with the purpose of figuring out what should stay and what needs to go on and get, we're going to have to get a little brainy with our faith and faith-y on our brain.

Part of wrestling is listening to God and trying to figure out what the absolute HECK God might be saying, if they're saying anything. And look, I know what some of you are thinking because it's the same thing I probably would have been thinking a few years ago. Or maybe your Religion Cop showed up.

RELIGION COP
This is such BS. She's going to talk about how she hears from God, and I am so sick to death of these ding-dongs yapping

about how they hear from God or God speaks to them, when in reality that stuff should put you in an institution. This is definitely going to be where she justifies doing whatever the heck she wants to do because "Holy Spirit revealed it" to her.

All I can say to that is your frustration is real. Not everyone gets a ram caught in a thicket or a descending dove. There are a million ways to have a conversation with God, with the Divine, and maybe it's less of a conversation and more of an experience. My hope is not to present a formula or rubric here, but rather a few leads for us as we try to find our footing amid disruption.

Nature

What is more quintessential than the God who created nature communicating through it? Water into wine, sassy donkeys, increasingly alarming plagues: nature is one of God's favorite megaphones. And I am so envious of the nature people. A friend of mine believes God speaks to her in the wind. What does God say? Wind noises only she can translate. Is that enough? It is for her. Another friend of mine saw some birds waddling down her driveway and knew they were a message from the Lord. But of course there's the science aspect to being in nature too. Endorphins, brain clarity, vitamin D. If God is who they say they are, this is a Creator who said, "I'm going to make the trees have a thing that when people touch them, it's going to make the people feel good. It's going to release chemicals in their brains to make them actually feel physically good." God is speaking the Konami Code* over

*For my non–video game nerds, the Konami Code is the famous cheat code in *Contra*: up-up-down-down-left-right-left-right-B-A. I love you, Ben Moon.

nature, whispering to us in breezes and healing us with herbs and lowering our anxiety when we touch grass. I would still like a word about cockroaches, however.

Others

This is when the Lord uses the witness and testimony of other people in your life to gently guide you. Maybe they are particularly susceptible to a word from Holy Spirit and they felt bestirred while reading a psalm, so they text you. Perhaps God had a message for you tucked away in a sermon or in another friend's processing as you walked with them. Sometimes this one does happen for me, but it's usually God telling my friend Retha to tell me to quit screwing around and write this book or my friend Erin N. asking me how I feel about something in my heart, which we both know is dumb, you can't feel anything in your heart.

Scripture

Jehovah Jireh lays the plans for your life out for you between the storied lines of the enslaved Hebrews, the ancient Israelites, and the Jews waiting for the deliverance of the Messiah, all found within the pages of the Bible. You can endlessly turn the gem and never tire of the discovery of God's word and truth laid out for your life in Scripture. I tried this once as a child and prayed for God to have a word for me wherever my Teen Study Bible opened. I hope God did not have a word for me from a certain passage in Ezekiel, which stated that Israel was like a sex worker who just loved big dangling donkey balls and horse seminal emissions (Ezek. 23:20—how's that for a proof text?). It feels important to mention this is when I found out what a seminal emission was exactly, and that horses could have them. Good for horses.

Prayer

I've always been slightly envious (in a holy way) of those who experienced God speaking to them in prayer. I knew a woman who seemed to have one of those genuine, honest-to-goodness telephone lines to God; she would have "a word" for people from her weekly prayer time. What was that about?! Where does one sign up for such a thing? But for me, prayer has always been just me sitting in my room, trying to stay awake or getting distracted by the internet or children. God's not speaking to me as much as God's probably waiting for me to get still for half a second.

The One-Man Band

God uses a special tactic with those special children, a method I've christened The One-Man Band. Imagine Bert from the original *Mary Poppins* is God, employing every method above and probably some extras to get my attention. Our Heavenly Father is up there really going to town: cymbals clanging, drums beating, horns tooting. One hand is on the nature button: "Meaningful waterfall moment, go." Holy Spirit's messing around in my dreams, my husband wants to talk about a conversation he's been having on Slack with one of his coworkers that relates to this book that keeps popping up in my Instagram ads. Somewhere in Canada, a podcaster says something into a mic that will be meaningful if my friend April texts me three times to listen to it. My eldest daughter comes home from her step-church (this is the church she goes to on Wednesday night, but not the church we all go to sometimes), eager to share all the things she's learned and show me the notes from the sermon, which happens to be about a thing that keeps coming up in my conversations or in my podcasts, but I am trying to play Two Dots?! And then, I show up to my Bad Church Ladies meeting, a very annoying tune playing in the back of my brain, and I say, "I cannot get this song out of my head, do you think it means something?" Meanwhile God cues the angels to start singing the "Hallelujah" chorus, which I will not hear with my ears but maybe I will in my heart? Jesus high-fives Peter and everyone goes out for a beer, congratulating themselves and wondering if it will be this hard again next time. It will, my guys. It will.

This is The One-Man Band.

So now that you might have an idea of how God speaks to you, it's time to get inside your brain: the seat of where you think about God, where your spirituality is formed, and how you start to ask your questions.

Let's go back to our little plot of land. The tendency here is for us to start building something with the same blueprint we had before. Because we know what that looks like. Simply rebuilding a "better" version of the things we know is seductive. And that's not always bad. But it's bad if it's the rote response. So, as we clean up the ash and sweep away the detritus, we need to remember our brains do not want us to do this. Those brains want cozy, familiar, and easy. And that is why it feels like we're running a marathon through molasses.

And that's just what's happening on the surface. As long as we've had a basic understanding of what the brain does, scientists have wanted to know how belief and our gray matter work together, if they do at all. Recent research proposes there's some interesting stuff going on in a part of the brain called the periaqueductal gray.

Where is it? No clue. But Dr. Michael Ferguson, a neuroscientist with the rare honor of holding simultaneous appointments at Harvard Medical School and Harvard Divinity School, explains it like this: "Our results suggest that spirituality and religiosity are rooted in fundamental, neurobiological dynamics and deeply woven into our neurofabric. We were astonished to find that this brain circuit for spirituality is centered in one of the most evolutionarily preserved structures in the brain."[5] Dr. Mike is saying there's evidence pointing to the idea that since the beginning of humanity, we've had the capacity for belief. Not only that, but the periaqueductal gray is associated with super compelling functions in relation to belief, such as fear conditioning (easy to see how that one could get exploited), pain modulation, altruistic behaviors, and unconditional love.

And this is all interesting, but to what end? I kind of have the same attitude as Seth Horowitz, a neuropsychologist at Brown University: "You list a bunch of places in the brain as if naming something lets you understand it."[6] I'm not a brain person, but I am a faith person, and it seems to me there are a few ways you can interpret this neurotheological information.

One is definitely panic. *Oh, s-word. Does this mean we made all this up in our heads? Is religion or God just a way we're dealing with our inevitable march toward the abyss, and our brain gaslights us so we're not paralyzed by despair?* It can get dark quickly!

Another is to ignore the mind-body connection altogether, which is kind of what we've been doing in evangelical circles for a while. Ask any girl who grew up in purity culture and is hyperaware of her breasts while also being surprised she has a chest at all. It's easier to just not think about the possibilities of what it could mean if our brain and our spirituality are tied up with one another. The devil you know, etc.

But here's what compels me. Our connection to God, our faith, this thing we're wrestling with, it lives in our bodies, it's housed in our brain—that beautiful hub that powers us, the one that is, if God is who God says they are, deeply personal. Fr. Ilia Delio, who holds the distinction of being a Franciscan monk AND having PhDs in historical theology and pharmacology, makes a great point: "Spirituality involves the brain. For the first time in human history, we are beginning to understand spiritual experience not as something apart from the physical human but rather bound up with human matter."[7] It's not floating ethereally, an abstract concept living in the conceptual world. It's flesh and blood. It's up there in our wrinkly brains, and we live it out through our hands and feet. Tangible and intangible, all at once.

A couple of years ago, an Italian docent named Irene clapped her hands at me from the opposite side of the Vatican Gallery of Maps. "Andiamo," she whispered, hurrying us along through corridors stuffed with absolutely priceless works of art; name an artist, and they are casually displayed along the hallways. As we mall-walked by, Irene pointed to one of the ancient Roman sculptures that, once proudly naked, was now modestly covered with a fig leaf. "Somewhere in the Vatican," she whispered, raising her eyebrow conspiratorially, "there's a drawer where all the little sculpture penises the popes broke off are just rolling around, waiting to be put back on."

Sadly, we did not have time to unpack that story as we raced to our appointment. Irene pulled her considerable strings to get us into the Sistine Chapel before it officially opened to the public, but we needed to hustle, thus the reason for flying past Matisse's *Madonna and Child, The School of Athens, Laocoön and His Sons,* the *Artemis of Ephesus* ("You see, they let her keep all her breasts, the cheeky popes!"). Finally, we stood breathless behind some very inconspicuous wooden doors and the Americans were again reminded not to talk or take pictures in the sacred space we were about to enter.

When you walk inside, it's almost as if God gently raises your chin with a God finger, the way your gaze unconsciously lifts to the ceiling. You can't help but immediately orient yourself to the most famous painting in history, *The Creation of Adam,* painted by Michelangelo.

We all know it. The languid Adam, waking to life, his hand barely raised in extension from his arm, his finger reaching, almost there. The tiniest of spaces between creation and Creator, speaking to the widest of chasms. Then another finger, this one so full of life, attached with strength to a vibrant arm, God's, wrapped in motion and a shroud and future creations waiting to take shape just behind him. Of course, art historians can dither about what exactly we're seeing, but the general consensus is we've stumbled upon our scene right before the divine breath, represented by the tips of fingers forever hovering in stasis.

I ignored the crick in my neck, as it felt disrespectful (maybe even bordering on lazy) to complain about sore muscles after simply looking up for five minutes when Michelangelo had to paint the dang thing in the same position for sixteen days. And he wasn't even really a painter. And it's considered one of the greatest works of all time. So I distracted myself by trying to remember the Easter eggs hidden in Michelangelo's work my art history professor lectured on fifteen years ago.

In 1990, an ob-gyn and amateur artist from Indianapolis, Indiana, named Dr. Frank Meshberger published a paper suggesting that Michelangelo's rendition of God in *The Creation of Adam* sat inside a shroud representing "a perfect anatomical illustration of the human brain in cross section."[8] A quiet pupil of anatomy (cutting up cadavers and looking at the insides of bodies at seventeen was not really socially accepted at the time), Michelangelo also studied the work of his frenemy, Leonardo da Vinci, whose notes reveal a deep understanding of the human body, so we know there's at least a precedent for something like a Renaissance master hiding a brain in plain sight within a painting of the creation narrative. Dr. Frank makes the case that not only does the image look like what casual brain observers like you and me know the brain looks like, it also includes parts of the brain that only someone with a working knowledge would be able to replicate. That around the shadowy edges where faraway figures lurk, Michelangelo deliberately painted the shadows of the Sylvian fissure and the optic chiasm. That God and the figure crooked in his other arm—Sophia, the personification of wisdom—together make the outline of the cingulate sulcus, a part of our brain that controls emotional responses to behavior. That the long blue fabric extending from the neck of the figure underneath God, who some art scholars think may represent Christ, is the vertebral artery. That the arm and leg poking out at the bottom are the pituitary stalk and the medulla, respectively. That Michelangelo very intentionally and by specific design placed God inside a human brain.

But why?

Dr. Frank's revelation sent the art and religious worlds into a tailspin. *What did it mean?* Everyone from museum curators to archbishops wanted to know. Michelangelo and Pope Julius, the pope who commissioned Mike to paint the ceiling in the first place, had famous beef, so one assumption was that the painter was simply giving Julius the middle finger by insinuating God was nothing more than a figment of his imagination. Which, to be fair, would have been an absolutely devastating burn, had it not been so subtle it took almost five hundred years for someone to notice.

It also didn't hold much water as a theory because Michelangelo himself was a religious guy who took his faith seriously. One might even say he took his faith more seriously than Julius himself. So a thinly veiled reference to God as the pope's imaginary friend would have also been a self-own.

The real problem was that Michelangelo wasn't around to ask. What was simply one of humankind's greatest paintings, inside of one of our most powerful centers of religion, representing one of our most enduring stories, was now a mystery. And everyone had their own interpretation. Michelangelo was a secret atheist. Michelangelo was trying to tell us God's greatest gift was our intellect. Michelangelo's thesis was that being made in the image of God meant being like-minded with God. Michelangelo was prophesying the Enlightenment. Michelangelo was secretly standing in solidarity with the scientists being tried for heresy in the Catholic church at the time.

This went on for the next twentyish years, both scholars and amateurs offering their theories, until another paper was published, this time by medical illustrator Ian Suk and neurosurgeon Rafael Tamargo, highlighting their discovery of another sixteenth-century neurotheological Easter egg in the Sistine Chapel.[9]

The force that compels your eyes upward when you enter the chapel causes you to skip several of the other ceiling panels. The first one is called *The Separation of Light from Darkness*, which depicts God doing just that: separating the light from the darkness as described in the Genesis 1 creation narrative.

The art historians who have dedicated their careers to just the Sistine Chapel have always been puzzled by this particular panel, specifically by God's neck, one of the last portions Michelangelo painted. Considering he spent his entire life studying the human body inside and out to masterfully depict it in his work, it was always confusing to reconcile why he missed so hard. On a portrait of God. At a focal point of the chapel. The anatomy is off, with weird bulges and shapes definitely not found on necks in general. The lighting is also strange for someone who deftly understood the interplay of light and shadow on a genius level.

Suk and Tamargo claim it's no accident at all, because when you lay God's throat and chest over anatomically correct images of the human spinal cord and brain stem, they match up perfectly.

What, exactly, is Michelangelo up to, putting a human brain stem where God's larynx goes?

A lot of time, space, and smarts separate us, but Michelangelo grew up like a lot of us, just a kid messing around with his friends, studying, and getting bored in church. It was evident pretty early on that he wasn't going to follow in his dad's government job footsteps, and by the time he was twenty-five, he had sculpted the *Pietà*. So same, but different.

But as his talent caught the eye of the wealthy and elite, he found himself rubbing elbows in the halls of religious power. The more he saw how the sausage got made in the church, the more he saw what was, at that time, a high point of corruption and exploitation from the religious leaders, and the more disillusioned he became. Michelangelo's life was also running parallel with what was a fascinating time for religion, with new ideas like how a person didn't need a priest or a church to commune with God—rather, they had that ability innately within them—which happened to be an official heresy of the Catholic church at that particular moment.

I wonder if Michelangelo considered 1 Corinthians 2:16, where Paul posits the rhetorical question "For who has known the mind of the Lord, so as to advise him?" (NET), which is Paul showing off a little because he's also quoting a passage from the Torah, from the scroll of Isaiah, one of the prophets. And the question Isaiah is asking here is part of a greater monologue extolling God's unknowability, God's mystery. "Who could ever have told GOD what to do or taught him his business? . . . So who even comes close to being like God? To whom or what can you compare him?" (Isa. 40:12–20).

"Who has known the mind of the Lord, so as to advise him?"

And for a long time, the answer to Isaiah's question was simply: no one. Only God was the possessor of God's Spirit, and, as Paul says earlier in his letter, the only person who can understand who they are is their own spirit (1 Cor. 2:11 NIV). Same with God. So no one can understand God because no one else has God's Spirit.

But when Paul writes to the Corinthians and quotes his predecessor, the question has a different answer on this side of the Testaments. Something has changed.

"Who has known the mind of the Lord, so as to advise him?" asks Isaiah from across the void.

Paul answers back, "We do, actually. We have the mind of Christ" (2:16 NIV).

When Michelangelo hid anatomically correct brains and voice boxes all over God's body, my interpretation is that he was reminding the six million people who gawk at his work every year:

The place where God speaks comes from you.

The ways through which God moves come from you.

The methods through which God is known come from you.

We have God's Spirit.

We were made in God's image.

We have the body of Christ.

We are the place where God dwells.

We have God's voice.

We have the mind of Christ.

The gifts of God for the people of God.

Michelangelo lovingly painted heresies onto the ceiling, perhaps, as he called his earlier anatomy studies to mind, pondering if it really was true. That God wasn't kept behind a golden wall, only accessible to those with theological instruction, good connections, and enough money. Just because the pope believed the people needed an intercessor between them and God, just because the bishops thought a Bible in everyone's common tongue was profane, just because the powers that be thought God was too other to be human, Michelangelo brushed reds and purples into the plaster and said, "Just because they say it, doesn't make it so."

I will lovingly paint another heresy for our own time: God isn't behind a golden wall, only accessible to those with seminary degrees, 401(k)s, and enough money. The questions you ask, the ways God speaks to you, your lived experience, and the deconstruction of your faith—these things are not evil or bad just because someone with a podcast mic decides you're a problem or a pastor from a big church in Texas says it's just an excuse for you to sin. Whatever version of faith those dissenters are protecting, it might not be yours anymore. So give them back the key and wish them well.

Just because they say it, doesn't make it so.

Our big, beautiful brains, where all our questions and doubts and cares and passions and hopes originate, are shared with Christ and created by God, where God's Spirit dwells. God wasn't in the field or the house when we burned it down. Maybe there were misconceptions or misunderstandings that died in the fire, but if you want God to, I believe God stays with us as we work our charred land, in whatever capacity God is welcomed, be it tentatively or with side-eye.

Those big, beautiful brains, pushing and pulling, desperately resisting the question marks in favor of comfort and safety. It's easier not to interrogate, not to search. It's simpler to keep moving along the long-established grooves. But if we have the mind of Christ, which Paul says we do, we also cannot help but be who we are. It's why the questions are surfacing anyway. We know we aren't made to skim these surfaces; we know it's not just a botched paint job on God's neck. We follow a thread of desperate hope that there is more.

There's something else here.

Maybe a seventeen-year-old Michelangelo dissected a human brain one night, and inside he saw God, not a threat. He let his questions lead him further into faith, deeper into discovery, and by the time he climbed the scaffolding, he was on a path to one day write the words:

> The prayers I make will then be sweet indeed,
> If Thou the spirit give by which I pray:
> My unassisted heart is barren clay,
> Which of its native self can nothing feed:
> Of good and pious works Thou are the seed,
> Which quickens only where Thou say'st it may;
> *Unless Thou show us to Thine own true way,*
> *No man can find it: Father! Thou must lead.*
> *Do Thou, then, breathe those thoughts into my*
>   *mind*
> By which such virtue may in me be bred
> That in Thy holy footsteps I may tread;
> The fetters of my tongue do Thou unbind,
> That I may have the power to sing of Thee,
> And sound Thy praises everlastingly.[10] (emphasis
>   added)

Look, it's disingenuous for me to tell you Michelangelo lived the rest of his life as some sort of Renaissance deconstructionist. His poetry isn't all a beautiful metaphor for God placing God's spark of life into us. He struggled. He agonized. This is the same guy who, when tasked later in life to paint *The Last Judgment* behind the altar of the Chapel, included a self-portrait in the limp, flayed skinsuit held by St. Bartholomew as he ascends to heaven. Going to be with God, maybe, but not necessarily in one piece.

Having the mind of Christ doesn't mean you get everything right. We are still human, still in the process of being made new. I know Religion Cop is sitting on your shoulder right now, telling you I'm full of s-word.

RELIGION COP

She's just telling you that you can do whatever you want and says it's fine because she has God's brain or whatever. Or maybe you just didn't have any faith to begin with.

I call bullshit.* Is it possible the questions come not because you're trouble, but because you see trouble? Could it be that you doubt not because you're wrong, but because something is wrong? Are you faithless, or are you faithful to something thicker than empty creeds and heartier than temporary power grabs? Are you poison, causing dissension and division, or are you truth serum?

I can't answer those questions for you, but neither can anyone else. But do not linger in them, because ultimately your options are limited. Red pill or blue pill? High heel or Birkenstock? You know there is something beyond an exclusionary, tight-fisted, power-hungry, limp "faith" hellbent on control at any cost so, as my friend Morgan says, "pick your medicine."

Beloved, trust God. Trust God's Spirit in you. Trust the questions fomenting in the marrow of your bones that feel like they will break you. They might, but you are being made new too. You don't have to prove your journey (drink) to anyone. God can speak to you just as easily as anyone else. You can breeze right by the fake officials who say you must have never believed anyway; they actually have no authority over you. They play keep-away with the keys to the kingdom, but the gates have always been unlocked.

It's not possible to deconstruct in a vacuum. It might be easier, but while we're contending with our brains, doing the dance of trying to be flexible and solid in all the right ways,

*Oh look at that, that just slipped in there.

there are other brains out there in the wild to deal with. Brains we love. Brains we live with. Brains that first stuck Felt Board Jesus on a Felt Board Cross. Brains that raised us. Brains we're married to.

It's easier to dismiss the criticisms of a pastoral TikTok critique. It's harder to navigate your relationship with someone you love who is concerned you're now definitely going to hell. And now, if you weren't on the fence about hell as a concept, you might think they would be too.*

Because a burned-out field looks like catastrophic damage to the untrained eye that has never seen a controlled burn. I truly believe, for the most part, when your wandering heart is added to some prayer list, it's from a place of genuine concern. No one wants to see someone they love get hurt, be ostracized, incur the wrath of the Almighty. If anything, it's almost a little encouraging. They still believe this expression of faith is where the words of life can be found, and they want to keep you within the fold.

When you've just begun to trust the work of God's Spirit, God's mind in you, it can be hard to not be understood. It can be hard to look across the table at someone who prayed the Sinner's prayer with you and say, "The reason I'm asking these questions is because I believed you when you told me about God. I believed what you said about Jesus. The radical gospel you taught me is what led me here."

But here's the thing. You can't change anyone else's mind but your own. Your brain is your brain. Your questions are your questions. As much as we want someone to see the same things we see, to spot the problems we spot, deconstruction is an individual process. What gets in my craw is not the same as what gets in yours. What breaks me will not break you. What

*Kinda hyperbolic, kinda not.

mends me will not mend you. Everyone is on their own time-line, working at their own speed. We have to trust that too.

Being a person of faith does not prohibit our questions. It does not erase our doubts. Our belief system does not have to exclude any part of us. In fact, it encourages all of us to come to the table in our freedom. We can hold the questions, the doubts, the skepticism, the cynicism, the parts that desperately want to believe, the corniness, the trust, the love, the hope. It all belongs in the wrestling ring. But that doesn't mean it—"it" being this wild, corny, beautiful, not-for-the-faint-hearted journey of faith (drink)—won't be hard.

PRESSURE
POINTS

What Makes Faith So Hard, and What Compels Me to Stay

Before the truth sets you free, it tends to make you miserable.

Fr. Richard Rohr, *Falling Upward*

Dear Erin,
  I hope this isn't presumptuous, but why the eff are we even doing this anymore?

Regards,
Liv

I do appreciate an email that gets right to the point.

Because I am a Person with a Faith Podcast, sometimes I get Internet Frangers (these are strangers who become friends) who are in the midst of also trying to figure out why this whole faith thing is so hard, and since it is, is it even worth it? And they inevitably ask some form of this question:

Why on earth are we still trying to do this? Why are we still trying to be Christians?

And it's a perfectly valid question, which is why I want to talk about our pressure points as the next part of our discernment process. As I hope you know by now, God is not afraid of your questions and, to the contrary, welcomes them. If you've spent some time confronting your questions, you are likely in touch with the ones that bring the most heat for you. This is how I have come to think of pressure points: where your deepest questions come to a head, and you must decide if you're going to stay with this thing called faith or call the whole thing off.

If questions are the simmering of a kettle on the stove, pressure points are when the water hits its boiling point, and the kettle starts screaming. And like a screaming kettle, our pressure points are simply too powerful to be ignored. They are the last straw, the final frontier, the fork in the road where we are pressed to decide: Is Jesus really, actually trustworthy? Am I missing something here, or is this issue too important to me to keep going any further? If I can't get over this, what's the point in even moving forward at all?

Everyone's pressure points are different. It could be hell. It could be how all "those people" voted for "that president." Maybe it's the problem of pain or why bad things happen to good people. For me, it was why most of the Christians I knew simply did not live as if their very beings had been wholly resurrected and instead decided to play in tiny sandboxes of politics and pettiness. And that included myself.

So why on earth are we still trying to do this? Because there are times when I would much prefer to just not do this whole dance with God. And people. And forget community, because people are the worst and sometimes Christians are the worst of all. Theology sucks. The Bible is too big and also too small. Christianity is too exclusive while gaslighting you to say it's so inclusive, it's too married to empire, it's perpetuated too many atrocities. There's supposed to be a God who created an ever-expanding universe, unbound by time and space, so other, so euphorically loving, so beyond what the natural mind could ever conceive, and for some reason we've decided to make that God punitive and small.

Dear Liv,

If you catch me on a good day, I can put my finger on my neck and feel the pulse of my ancestors, people who carried a faith from across the sea, who bounced around the southeastern US, who buried babies and built houses and lived and died. Who in some way passed a faith all the way down to me. I don't know how you first stumbled upon God, Liv, but maybe your finger can find the pulse too.

Some days I can wake connected to the force of Divine Love which calls to me from my dishwashing, my clothes folding, my list-making to come and be still. Some days my bones are alight with radical empathy, with open-handed generosity, with unrestricted love, things I cannot bring to the table on my own, gifts I've received from God, who I am learning loves to give curious gifts. Some days I can feel God's Spirit in me.

Do the days threaten to crush you, Liv? They do me, but some days when I take the time to stop and breathe in this created world with its kindness and my children's freckles and resurrection and hand-rolled pasta, I think God might be real. When I read a story that flickers longing in my heart, I think God might love us. When I burrow cold toes under Ben Moon's warmth and he absentmindedly cradles my ankle, I think God might like us.

When I get distracted, some days I can feel a tug, a reminder, Holy Spirit's hand resting gently on my shoulder, guiding and directing me, showing me all the ways Jesus is moving in my world, inviting me to be a part if I want. *Look at how I love this place. Come love it with me.* Some days I end in a rapturous love affair with God, confident in my purpose, deeply possessed of the knowledge and understanding that I am beloved, and nothing I can say or do or think or be will ever change that.

I am God's beloved. The truest thing about me is that I am God's beloved.

Are you like me, Liv (and your email indicates that you are)? I can make the case to myself that, of all the religions and faith expressions and spiritualities I've studied and investigated throughout my life, I am infatuated by Jesus: his teachings, the way he upended cultural norms, the radical and revolutionary rumor that he actually rose from the dead and not only that, but he's making it possible for everyone to brush the grave dirt off. I know even though it is weird as hell to say I have a personal relationship with a resurrected rabbi from the first century, I do believe that relationship begets abundant life in my life: not blessings of material wealth or good health, but the living presence of that euphorically loving, unbound-by-time-and-space Divine Mystery. And I can make the case to myself that no amount of Christian fascism or religious misogyny or bad theology can ever be enough to make me not want to follow that my whole life, to live firmly and confidently in God. To trust that burning it all down just purifies and refines, and I am not afraid of what is not true anyway.

But if you catch me on an off day, Liv, it's a different story.

These are the days when I think lighting a match and burning it all to the ground is letting the Christian-industrial complex off easy. Mustering up the energy to be angry seems like a waste of time, because what good would it ultimately do? If this is what it means to be a part of God's family, where are my emancipation papers? I see suffering in the world and trace it back, often not very far, to those who share my historical faith, often in what they believe is some sort of twisted service to that faith, and I want to scream all the worst words into a pillow as a prayer, if I bother with prayer at all.

I ping between pure rage at a God who would allow such a hellscape to exist without seemingly bothering to intervene and pure rage at a people who would claim belief in a rabbi like Jesus and perpetuate such a hellscape. The love and affection I feel for God is gone, and what remains is hostility, followed by panic, topped with apathy. *Look at what you made. Look at what we do to each other. Look how we do it in your name, to show you how much we love you. This is how we think you receive love. How messed up is that?*

If I can believe in God on those days, I do not believe God is good or paying attention. God certainly can't be doing both. Liv, there are days I do not believe in God. I do not believe Jesus is God's Son, and if he's not God's Son, then what are we doing exactly? I do not believe, and I do not want anyone to help me in my unbelief. I do not love God, if God is God, and I do not think God loves me. In fact, I do not even want to love God, because if this (*gestures wildly*) is what God is doing with God's time, I'm not interested.

I try not to engage with people on those days, Liv.

But one thing I've learned throughout this process is I must tell the truth, mostly to myself.

What Liv doesn't know is that telling the truth is hard for me, because I do not have a great track record with being honest.

147

When you're a theater major while also being a career drama queen, you have a lifelong membership to the Stretching the Truth Club, ranging from fun exaggerations that make the story better to complicated lies you need to keep straight to stay out of jail for a weekend. One of the great stories in our family lore is the time I lied about "totally understanding" seventh grade algebra and how I "definitely didn't need a tutor," but when report card time came, I made a 63, which was failing, which was bad. And in order to hide this deception from my parents, I needed to fake sick.

Faking sick is an art, and it takes a subtlety not recognized by most seventh graders. Their instinct is to go with a measurable illness with visual cues. Listen up, young truth stretchers: a headache is always the ticket. It requires zero acting skills (you simply close your eyes and pretend as though all light and sound render you nauseous), its intensity cannot be gauged by an outside source like a thermometer, and it has the potential to be so powerful, over-the-counter drugs cannot overcome it. A bonus is that there's no timetable attached to it; you never have to be headache-free for twenty-four hours before engaging in important social events.

This last bit was important because if I faked sick, I could "forget" my report card in my locker, thus postponing my punishment for lying about not needing help, now skirting the truth about the report card (and the failing thing was going to be a situation at this point too) from my parents until after the seventh grade Valentine's Dance. This was the most important social event of the season, and the fit was fire, as the kids say or once said by the time this book goes to print.*

*I have been informed I am still woefully behind.

Earlier that month, my mother and I had combed the racks at Dillard's and found the most elegant red silk dress with a tone-on-tone embroidery, short because Wilson women have incredible legs and delicate ankles, and we don't mind saying so, thank you very much. Somehow, we managed to uncover a puffy red headband from Claire's, perfectly color matched with the dress, along with dazzling dangly earrings that made me feel like I was basically a cover model for *YM Magazine*'s prom edition. Bare legs were out of the question because it would be cold, so we layered opaque white tights (this was weird, but it made sense at the time) under the most grown-up shoes I'd ever been allowed to wear: red, strappy, with a little heel. Was I Fancy from the Reba McEntire "Fancy" music video? Probably. You could not tell me anything in that outfit. I tried it on a million times, primping and prepping for my second kiss with my boyfriend on the gym floor of Canyon Junior High School while TLC's "Waterfalls" inevitably played over the loudspeaker. I was going to hot roll and tease my hair, which I considered a chic yet effortless style choice. The Valentine's Dance was about glamour, it was about passion, it was about holding sweaty hands and barely touching each other on the waist and/or shoulders while you moved in a circle and the Electric Slide and romance.

I, along with everyone else in the seventh grade, was very much looking forward to the seventh grade Valentine's Dance.

If you are not the child of a teacher, you might not know this, but you can't get away with anything, particularly if you are the child of a teacher in a small town. Never mind my Oscar-worthy performance to the nurse, who was convinced enough to actually call my mother. Never mind that my mother actually took me home and put me to bed with

Tylenol and a cold compress. I could not believe my plan was actually working, but pride cometh before the fall. Mothers always know and it wasn't long until it dawned on her that today was report card day for the junior high, and she had not seen mine. Caught in my web of lies, I attempted several strategies, hoping to salvage my chances of going to the dance.

I tried begging, threats of love removal, bribery. At one point I believe I told my mother I would "just miss my senior prom" if she and my father would let me go to the Valentine's Dance. But I was grounded. Not only that, but I was also grounded for the whole weekend. So, I was going to miss the Valentine's Dance AND my Sunday school class trip to Chili's.

Yea, though I walk through the valley of the shadow of death . . . however, I was comforted not by staff nor by rod.

The way my mother tells it, I "fell to my knees" and "wailed" and at some point, I began throwing that red dress and those red shoes into their bedroom, screaming (it was probably just enunciation but that's showbiz, baby), "I guess I won't be needing these anymore!"

I think that's when they added on the part about writing the sentence "I will be totally truthful at all times" one thousand times before I was ungrounded.

I've lied about speeding tickets, where I was with boys, where I wasn't with boys, where money went, how that dent got there, and why that assignment didn't get turned in on time. I've exaggerated stories, stretched already tall tales to make stories more entertaining, lived so deeply in fantasies even I was convinced they were true. I've probably misremembered a good 30 percent of the stories I've shared here. I've told lies of omission, white lies, suppressed information, told half-truths, prevaricated, misrepresented, and been just plain deceitful.

And every time, EVERY TIME, I get caught. I pay a price. And it is always painful. Even more painful than sitting in your living room on a Friday night when all your friends are at the seventh grade Valentine's Dance. And for what? What was the point? Just tell your parents you don't understand quadratic functions. You'll get a tutor, you'll pass algebra, you'll get to kiss a little and have some Southwestern Eggrolls after church on Sunday. It's just not that big of a deal.

So, as I've grown, I've tried my best to be as honest as possible, even when the truth feels hard or uncomfortable, even when the truth feels like it might kill me. The truth never kills. It's pretending to believe a lie you know is wrong that will kill you.

Earlier in our time together, I mentioned a quote misattributed to Carl Sagan, who I am certain would take umbrage with being included in this book: "If it can be destroyed by the truth, it deserves to be destroyed by the truth." It's a very good thought, and even if Sagan didn't write it, I think it describes his ethos. The quote is actually from a science fiction novel called *Seeker's Mask* by P. C. Hodgell: "That which can be destroyed by the truth, should be."[1]

Not that I would try to place thoughts in the heads of either Sagan or Hodgell, but this has always struck me as a very spiritual concept, a way to get to the heart of what really matters in faith, to cut all the fluff and feathers away.

I think about Galileo, who spent time in prison for daring to suggest maybe the sun doesn't revolve around the earth. While the religious authorities assumed such a concept would destroy the understanding of God's creation of the earth as the center of the universe, it blew the roof off how small we made God. If a solar system where the sun revolves around the earth is destroyed by the truth, it should be.

I think of the survivors of church abuse, who were wounded in the name of control and power. When they brought their stories to those who could help them, the truth destroyed the reputations of those who honored God in the light but who twisted their authority into something that looks more like the devil. If the "integrity" of a person or an institution is destroyed by the truth, it should be.

If an inerrant Bible is destroyed by the truth, it should be.

If what we've always been taught about who's in and who's out is destroyed by the truth, it should be.

If hidden budget line items and callous hearts and secret sins can be destroyed by the truth, they should be.

I think about Jesus (my friend—on the good days), who carefully and patiently unlocked the doors to freedom and Divine Love while denouncing all the clever ways his people had sidestepped true intimacy with God. If a religious system that is good news to only a few people is destroyed by the truth, it should be.

Sagan and Hodgell and Galileo and survivors of church abuse and, while I dislike saying definitive things about Jesus's inner thought life, Jesus would (probably) say: Good. What good is a sweater that doesn't keep you warm? What good is a structure built to protect a lie? What good is a foundation stone that leads to destruction?

Of course, this is terrifying for a lot of reasons. When you tell the truth you run the risk of pulling up a foundation stone that causes everything to crumble. You put yourself in a position of vulnerability because the structures placed around a lie can protect you. You pull a thread; what if the whole sweater comes unraveled?

Good.

Pull the thread.

Burn it down.

Tear it apart.

It wasn't doing its job anyway.

Back to my email to Liv.

Liv, sometimes when I'm not annoyed by the Bible, I go over to the Gospel of John. He quotes Jesus as saying, "If you continue to follow my teaching, you are really my disciples and you will know the truth, and the truth will set you free" (John 8:31–32 NET). We, the reluctant Christians, love to pull that quote out of context and gaze lovingly at it, but it's situated in the middle of an awkward conversation Jesus is having with a crowd of confused people. He's desperately trying to get them to see he's serious about being sent from God, that he's speaking the truth about who he is and what he's bringing to the table, but they think they know better. These religious people are so certain their interpretation of God is the truth, they can't see what's in front of them. "We are the descendants of Abraham. We are God's chosen people. God is our father!"* And let's tell another truth here: these people are primed to see Jesus. They've been waiting and watching. If we read stupidity or malicious intent into their frustrations here, it's because we have the benefit of hindsight. But they want the truth. We have a lot in common with them, don't we?

So Jesus, who often has a habit of being maddeningly mystifying on first read, lays it out clearly:

> "If God were your father," said Jesus, "you would love me, for I came from God and arrived here. . . . He sent me. Why can't you understand one word I say? Here's why: You can't handle it. . . . I arrive on the scene, tell you the plain truth,

---

*I'd like to acknowledge here that sometimes when we read the Gospels and talk about "religious leaders" or have all snide remarks and raised eyebrows toward the Pharisees, we can easily slip into an anti-Semitic attitude, casting them as the villains. It's probably a good exercise to interrogate the ways we label these biblical characters and speak of them regarding their merit as leaders, not fellow image-bearers.

and you refuse to have a thing to do with me. . . . Anyone on God's side listens to God's words. This is why you're not listening—because you're not on God's side." (John 8:42–47)

It's important to acknowledge that by the end of this conversation, the crowd actively attempts to murder Jesus. So now you may read malicious intent. And if you dropped Jesus into the twenty-first century, I can't see this interaction going any differently, including the murder part. If you eavesdrop on my personal heart-to-hearts with Jesus, there's a good bit of overlap. Because let me tell you what people do not like to hear: the truth, when it contradicts something they've already set up as truth in their brains. And I am first in line, Liv.

Truth can be easy and simple. It can be lovely and light, and on those days we count the freckles and practice resurrection and cook the pasta and warm the toes.

But there are truths that claw your back to shreds when you carry them. Cold truths that freeze you out. They afflict, they agitate, they disturb. They are not particularly comforting.

And yet this is Jesus we're dealing with here, so anchoring every truth, a ten-million-ton teaspoon of a neutron star, is radical, desperate hope.

If I could answer your question about why we're still even bothering with this whole thing, I'd distill the conundrum down to this: We are baptized in hope, and we are compelled to tell the truth.

At some point all those words—hope, truth, love, faith—kind of run together as vaguely inspirational ideas meant to spur us onward toward a general concept of being nicer. But when you drill down, Liv, it feels like telling the truth and having hope are two almost diametrically opposed concepts, and attempting to hold both in your body at the same time is enough to drive anyone to the absolute brink.

If telling the truth is crucial to being connected to God, if Jesus is right when he claims to be the truth, then I must share that I often see hope as an exercise in futility. When I observe the world around me, hope is the last thing that makes logical sense. I want to tap Martin Luther King Jr. on the shoulder in heaven and ask, "Do you really believe the arc of the universe bends toward justice? Even now?" I remember someone in a high school English class quoting Anne Frank from her diary (Lord, I cannot believe we make the diary of a teenager required reading), something about how inspirational Anne is because she believed, against all the evidence presented to the contrary, that people are really good at heart. This was a lovely sentiment to ruminate on until Colby Currie shouted from across the room, "Yeah, but she's dead."

That made Mrs. P mad, but Colby was telling the truth. She is dead. All her hope for humanity and her faith in the goodness of others didn't play out. She died at the hands of the Nazis and her innermost thoughts are questions on a test for freshman English classes forever and ever amen.

Hope is a reckless investment: the stakes are high and if things go south, you're in a bad place. And it is beyond easy to sink into the feather bed of hopelessness. To disconnect my heart and my spirit and my body from this flaming garbage truck of a world, to unhitch myself from the risk of faith at all and put my energy into protecting myself and my people from the truth of the matter: no one is coming to save you, and you can only trust yourself.

But then.

But then, but then, but then.

We can sink as far as we want, but the flaming garbage truck is never the end of the story. As much as the ache of the world is true, there is also resuscitating hope putting its breath in the lungs of truth and watching them inflate. And I think when Christians talk about hope, we tend to think they mean the pearly-gates-New-Jerusalem-future kind. But Jesus didn't say "abundant life when you get to heaven" or "abundant next life." Just "abundant life." Here. Now. And no one will be honest about the fact that telling the truth and walking in active hope is damn near impossible.

Because as a global faith, particularly in Western cultures, we've stopped telling the truth. The truth about what Jesus said, about who we are, about how we are supposed to take care of people, about what we're supposed to stand for, about what we're supposed to love. We've ignored, gaslit, rejected, or buried the truth and asked everyone to just be hopeful in a fantasy ungrounded in reality. Or we've decided to stay sitting upright at the cold table of judgment, criticizing anyone who dares to imagine a different way.

I get trapped in these patterns when I forget the actual bonkers nature of what we're saying we believe in here with Jesus. Like he told the crowd in John 8, he's saying he's offering a life without death, and besides that, a way of living that speaks to the humanity of every single person. When I really remember this is not about budget meetings or interpretations of Scripture, when I go back to pre-empire, weird Jesus who said strange things like "drink my blood and eat my flesh" and wanted us to love our enemies, I cannot shake it. Maybe you can, Liv. I'm not the one who can decide that for you.

I would love more than anything to extract myself from what feels like a fruitless exercise in longing expectation for love to triumph over hate. It would save me a lot of emotional capital at the very least. But dammit, I cannot shake the way the Gospels systematically blow up the idea that only the put-together and the fully articulate can be with God. How only the well or the rich or the powerful have access to God. I cannot look away from Jesus touching people considered to be unclean, Jesus inviting those that society deemed unfit, Jesus defying space and time and physics to show his love. The story of an expansive God compacting every bit of God's nature into a fragile, vulnerable infant. How it's true that love matters when it's honest, or to quote Paul, "No matter what I say, what I believe, and what I do, I'm bankrupt without love" (1 Cor. 13:3). How there's no denying that when you see someone, even yourself, in their belovedness, it can change who they are, how they live, and their purpose in the world. I cannot stop looking at the cracks where the light breaks free.

That's why the eff I'm even doing this anymore, Liv.

No matter how hard it tries, bleak, despondent truth cannot kill hope. And it does try, Liv. You need to know it's going to try really hard.

If we apply this to our burned-out piece of land, this truth treatment begins to extract hidden toxins from the soil. If it can be destroyed by the truth, it deserves to be. For God's sake, let it be. While we were distracted by whatever was happening on the surface, contaminants leached into the soil and acted like fertilizer for the crops we never wanted to grow. These are the places where our sacred imagination and our sanctified common sense are bereft, where we've been so beaten down, we no longer remember why we loved what we loved. Where the cuts of trying to overcome the harsh reality of what we see with our own two eyes just bleed and bleed and never heal. Where we can't envision the unrelenting truth dancing in time with functional hope. If we don't remedy the soil, if we don't address these pressure points, if we don't tell the truth about them, whatever we end up planting on our little plot of land will not be long for this world.

And in the spirit of telling the truth, Liv, I know this seems overwhelming and time-consuming. It is both those things. But working through these aspects of our faith is the freelance project of our lives. This is the process and invitation of walking with God, and that work together is composing an opus. You identify one toxin, you and Holy Spirit figure out where you land on something, and another one pops up. Or two at once. It may feel like they're all coming at you at the same time. Every critical thinker has, at some point, unearthed an aspect of what they were taught, brushed the mud and dirt away, examined it from all angles, researched it, talked about it, reconsidered it, and tried to figure out what to do with it. Maybe with a new perspective, maybe with the same perspective, but they did the work.

They moved toward the truth, baptized with hope.

And, if I may, let me just acknowledge how difficult it is to name truths within a religious structure that doesn't always want truths to be named. Of course, #NotAllChurches and #NotAllPastors and #NotAllParents. But because Christianity shows up in many different iterations, you do see high-control variations where truth-telling is not only ridiculed, it's considered dangerous and evil. You might be threatened with expulsion, or maybe that punishment could extend to your whole family. So you learn to conform for the sake of belonging because belonging means safety. I've done it, Liv, and maybe you have too.

There's also the aspect of what might be on the other side of the answers, right? Maybe you don't want to know how the Scripture sausage was made. Maybe looking closely at how the Sermon on the Mount convicts you of your priorities or the Year of Jubilee makes the way you spend your money or how you live your online life a little awkward. Maybe questioning the existence of hell means someone calls you a heretic and you don't want that. Maybe ending up in a place without solid answers makes you nervous after living in certainty for so long and that is uncomfortable.

Even just the act of identifying and naming the toxin out loud is powerful. Because that indoctrination goes deep, and you don't always realize the hold it has on you. And when you say it out loud, you finally know God's not actually sitting up there with a thunderbolt (that is Zeus, and he's a false god, sorry to the ancient Greeks reading this), waiting for you to tentatively say, "I am wondering if everything in the Bible is literally true and if not, does that mean all of Christianity is a lie?" There is an innate fear in leaching out these toxins, I know. It's that same fear from when you were younger and you said something someone considered dangerous or evil, so you learned to keep your questions to yourself.

But whoever that was, whoever that is, they are not in charge here. They do not get to tell you what's evil. They do not define dangerous. And it takes courage to push through that programming. It requires real inner work, but it's worth the challenge. Because if you continue letting whoever that is control your spiritual life, you'll keep getting what you've been getting. I don't know what is for you, but for me, it was confusion, frustration, shame, and fear.

Okay, so that is the truth. But also, there is hope, yes? Yes. After the poison is removed, we baptize that land in hope, baby.

Even if you have a complicated relationship with Scripture at the moment, it's interesting to see Jesus himself in fearless search for pollution. In his conversations with people like Photine, Nicodemus, and Zacchaeus, there's a real tenderness for those who are naming where they are stuck and asking good-faith questions, for people who are open to pulling unnatural chemicals from the soil and, even with hesitation or a little bit of fear, letting the floodgates open and engulfing the land with the expectation that it's all real.

He had some less-than-tender words for the folks who refused to honor those questions and instead used the weapon of self-righteous inflexibility to shame and isolate, to consolidate power for their own benefit. Even Jesus himself, as Brennan Manning says in *The Ragamuffin Gospel*, "was victorious not because he never flinched, talked back, or questioned, but having flinched, talked back, and questioned, he remained faithful."[2] And all being faithful means is having the gumption to keep working, honestly and hopefully, at your little plot of land.

The only way to access real hope is through telling the truth. And hope, by definition, looks stupid, feels foolish, and seems flimsy as a strategy. I think this is some of what Paul meant when he talks about how God chose the foolish things of the world to shame the wise. It is borderline embarrassing to watch the venom drip from your land while everyone else is pretending their land is thriving. The truth is you'll experience defeat and heartbreak and cynicism and days and weeks and years of throwing in the towel, only for God to throw it right back at you.

When the disciples put Jesus's body in the tomb, the truth of the matter was that he was dead. Whatever he told them, whatever promise he made, whatever visions were dreamed up, they got tucked away next to a broken and still body. Yes, they'd seen another body rise, another soul gasp back into flesh, but the one who made that happen was the one currently lifeless.

Liv, if you've had someone you love die, you know the way everything in you bottoms out, how the future immediately narrows, how your heartbeat betrays you. If you just reach far enough, you could grasp them back. If you could squeeze past space for a breath, make a bargain, rewind time just this once, and then you swear you'll never ask for anything again. You grapple for a tether where there is none.

I imagine that's how the disciples felt when they laid Jesus on the slab of rock, promising through tears to be back soon, to give what was left of him a proper burial. As they walked back in the truth of their reality, the hope level was nonexistent. It was bad enough he wasn't the Messiah; their friend was dead.

There was not an option for hope. Not an inkling. Not a whisper. Not the tiniest crack.

And then.

And then.

And then.

He was the tether all along.

It's not presumptuous, Liv, to ask why we're doing any of this. I can't answer it for you. But for me, if this is true, if Jesus offers nothing less than a love for us embodied in resurrection hope, then we do not have to be afraid of our bad days, of the days we can't believe. We do not have to diminish our pain. We do not have to pretend the poison isn't there. We can speak full-throated truth because nothing, absolutely nothing is going to stop hope from getting out of the grave.

I've long let go of most of my need to be right, or first, or best (or maybe more accurately, I will, with God's help). I am not certain about much, but if the resurrection is a trustworthy narrative, it extends a question back to us.

We've been asking the question: Why, looking at what we have as far as truth right now, would we want to do this?

Maybe a better question is: Why, glimpsing what might be possible if it's true what they say about the Easter story, would we not?

And that, for me, Liv, is the truth.

Regards,
Erin

Your Unsoothed Heart
Is Your Most Powerful Weapon

The fiercest anger of all, the most incurable, is that which
rages in the place of dearest love.

Euripides, *Medea*

"For a fun little exercise, pick a day before we meet again,
and I'd like for you to keep a list of all the things that anger
you—big and small. Write them down without judgment or
examination. Don't look at the list again until we can look
at it together. Okay, bye!"

My spiritual director disappeared from the Zoom call, and
I saw myself in the black reflection of my screen. I had just
spent the hour in a frenzy, mad about this and that.

"I know anger is a secondary emotion, but I don't know
what's underneath it," I said to her earlier in the call, attempting to sound smart by parroting something my coun-
selor mother had said once.

My spiritual director knew it was an attempt and countered
with, "What does it mean that it's a secondary emotion?"

It took everything in me not to roll my eyes. But I did the assignment.

When we came back to the Zoom call the next month, my spiritual director got the full spectrum of my existential crisis, no matter how petty or important.

"Read them out to me. Remember how you felt when you wrote them down."

"I'm angry no one moved the laundry over and now it smells like mildew. I'm mad I'm being willfully misunderstood in a social situation. I'm furious at a punk seventh grade boy who would benefit from being drop-kicked into the sun. Another (another another another another) Black man was killed today at a traffic stop for no reason at all. Just no reason. People I love are idiotic or racist or both. Some guy left us a one-star review on Apple Music with a warning that our podcast is heretical and dangerous, and I have a sneaking suspicion it's this bro podcaster who loves to troll us. A friend's child came out and her parents are acting like she raised him to be a serial killer. I saw the unhoused guy who gives me a thumbs-up on my way into work getting jostled and uprooted by the cops today, his sleeping bag rudely thrown into the street. The replies on Beth Moore's recent tweet about Donald Trump make me want to dox someone. Nancy in my DMs is being a real so-and-so, which makes me madder, because I kind of hate using pejoratives for women or for anyone, but she is making it so hard for me. Billionaires are honestly ruining the planet and they weirdly have the power to save it, but they just . . . don't. A coworker's dad has cancer. Someone used the last of my shampoo but had the audacity to put the empty bottle back in the shower, so I didn't know it was gone until midway through what ended up being a cold shower, because of living with girls. I popped a tire, which threw my whole day off, and I'm also mad at myself for being mad because some people have real problems. The nightly doomscroll revealed global and local injustices I have no power to influence in the slightest. Also, I lost the Wordle today. And yeah, I'm mad at myself for being mad about Wordle of all things when the world is what it is right now."

I looked up from my notebook. She was listening with her head cocked to the side, and when she realized I was finished, she looked into the camera, which had the effect of looking into my eyes, and said, "Yes. All very valid."

I didn't know it then, but I was draining the soil the tiniest bit.

As you examine and name the places where someone tried to protect you from the truth, where you weren't honest with yourself, or where the truth was deliberately obscured from you, you might feel some things. As you uncover what it's like to begin listening to Holy Spirit for yourself and not having that mandated for you in what may or may not be intentional or unintentional manipulation, another, different emotion can rise to the surface.

My siblings in Christ, this is what we call rage.

Truth has a way of allowing space for anger, and it will inevitably open your eyes to a wide range of things to be perpetually pissed about, so that, if you wanted, you could walk around all the time with a giant flame coming out of your skull. Examples include but are not limited to: being told only old White Dutch men understand how to interpret the Bible, church is the only safe place to encounter God, old people should be blindly respected, Jesus would be down with Christian nationalism. Truly, we could go on.

And those of us who grew up evangelical have a complicated relationship with anger, don't we?

We've got all this preconditioning about how we should NOT be angry in the first place, and there are certain ways we can be angry, and listen, if you're a White woman like me, we can't even begin to understand the ways our BIPOC sisters have had to manage their anger out in the world, lest they get a label unfairly fixed on them, which will probably happen anyway.

And then there's just the question of what we can get angry about. After all, the Bible has a lot to say about anger.

James 1:20 says the anger of man does not produce the righteousness of God. He also says we're supposed to be slow to anger, which I usually forget in the process of being quick to anger.

Ecclesiastes talks about how anger lodges in the heart of fools, but I can compartmentalize my various personalities pretty well, so what if it lodges in just one of my hearts?

Paul says love doesn't get angry, but then explain why I find myself counting to ten when the children who came from my body steal spoons from the kitchen and never return them? Paul also wrote in a letter to the Galatians that he wishes the people who were confusing his friends would castrate themselves, which feels like something an angry person would say, so maybe Paul had some anger issues as well (Gal. 5:12).

I personally subscribe to the Ephesians 4:26 biblical mandate: "Be angry and do not sin" (NET). Here we have an interesting directive. I can be angry, and I can also not sin at the same time? So you're saying if I do this correctly, I can rage sinlessly? Let's go.

How would one be angry and still not cross over into sin? I believe you'd have to be angry about the things God and Jesus are angry about.

Jesus got mad a good bit. Maybe that seems weird, but I think it's because he was consistently telling the truth while putting active hope into the world. He saw the places where truth and hope stopped coexisting, and it chapped his hide. So, if we're going to take a trip into how to be angry while ideally doing it for the right reasons, let's look at what exasperated our Lord.

Dumb-A Religious BS

If Jesus got in someone's chili, it was folks who engaged in Dumb-A Religious BS. Religious leaders of his day* were always asking him about the law or trying to catch him in a trap, and not only that, but they also made up rules and held the Word of God hostage, denying freedom to God's people. And boy, did this frustrate the dog out of Jesus, because these were the people with their noses in the Scripture scrolls. They were supposed to know better. They were supposed to recognize him. We get a lot of scenes in the Gospels where Jesus goes ten toes down with these religious leaders, telling them they are of the devil and also their insides are maggoty, which is 100 percent something I would love to say to a lot of people, but Holy Spirit says no.

The Least of These Being Ignored

One thing Jesus never did was big time anyone. And he had every reason. The man was popular: he was a teacher with a following, constantly being pawed at and asked for his time. *Can you heal this person for me? My dog is sick and I love that dog so much. My brother has a demon or maybe he's just a jerk, can you come see?* So our guy frequently slipped away for private prayer and, I also assume, a nap. Let Jesus nap.

---

*Again, important to pay attention to the merits of their leadership skills, not their personhood.

It would have been easy for him to "accidentally" not see the bleeding woman. He could have gone about his day, knowing she was healed, knowing she believed, and letting that be enough. There's no reason for him to admonish the disciples for keeping kids from coming to see him. You think our society today is anti-kid? These people were making kids work full-time for the family at eight and marrying them off by twelve, okay? It would have been perfectly within cultural norms for Jesus to ignore the kiddos. It would've been very simple for Jesus to walk right on by Zacchaeus, not acknowledge him, not speak to him, never take the time to eat a meal in his home. Again and again, we see Jesus's anger flicker into action when those in the margins do not get the attention they deserve. And that tells us something about his character: every person has worth and value and we're not going to act like they don't. Not in this house.

Roadblocks to Faith

Everyone's favorite example of Jesus's anger: flipping over the tables in the temple. This one gets thrown around as a rage-against-the-machine-free card for being mad about whatever you want, but let's look at it a little deeper, because it's not just Jesus going Incredible Hulk on some money changers for funsies. During the Second Temple period, anyone who lived in Roman-occupied territory used Roman coins to conduct business, everywhere except the Jewish temple. Part of the temple procedure was purchasing an animal (the type depended on your tax bracket) to be killed and used in place of you for the atoning of your sin. As followers of Jewish law, the Jews could not bring graven images into the temple, which included Roman coins because of the portrait of Caesar they stamped on the front of every piece. Cue the moneychangers. They would take your Roman coins in exchange for some shekels, which were permitted for use in the temple complex, because no graven images. But businessmen that they were, they'd charge a little extra and keep some for themselves. Which is cool, because people need to eat and it's an honest day's work, until they started charging a lot extra and keeping a lot for themselves.

Jesus Christ our Lord and Savior did not like this business plan.

Anytime someone puts up a roadblock to connecting with Jesus, whether that's financial or spiritual or mental or physical, Jesus is right behind them, ready to burn that mother to the ground. Everyone loves it when Jesus takes up the whip and turns over the tables in the temple courtyard because giving this incident a cursory glance feels like a permission slip for "righteous anger."

But often (and I'm preaching to myself here), we assign our anger the label of *righteous* when it's really self-righteous. And we have such good practice mislabeling we might be able to pull it off if no one's looking closely. Best I can tell, Jesus's anger here is on behalf of oppressed people who are being taken advantage of. They are not being allowed to exercise their faith unless they go over this roadblock, which some do not have the ability to do. They don't have enough money to engage in temple worship, so they must skip the rite all together. Jesus does not like that someone is making a buck off the backs of God's most vulnerable people. When Jesus starts making whips in the temple courtyard, he's on the cusp of tearing down all the roadblocks for everyone to get to God: temple veils and purity laws and Gentile restrictions, so this Mickey Mouse BS had to go ASAP.

Jesus cursed a fig tree. Jesus got irritated. Jesus told one of his best friends, "Get behind me, Satan" (Matt. 16:23

NIV). Jesus's anger did not take away from his divinity, if we believe he was divine. If anything, it seems as if Jesus's anger was guided by his divinity and rooted in his humanity.

So when we hold up these examples and place them over the anger we feel about our particular pressure points, it's like we can hear the beginning refrain of "What a Friend We Have in Jesus." For me, it felt (it feels!) as if everywhere I turned, there was another complex system created by nefarious societal structures meant to uplift a certain subset of humanity while mashing a giant thumb down on everyone else. And we were all trapped in it. And these systems were hidden! But also in plain sight! And we were all complicit! But also victims! And I had privileges! But also disadvantages! And my God, my God, the sheer number of problems in the world. In my country alone. And don't forget the trolling bro podcasters. I'VE GOT TO HAVE AN OUTLET FOR ALL THIS ANGER SO I DO NOT SIN, PAUL. HOW ARE WE MANAGING TO NOT SIN, PAUL?

I cannot tell you to lean into your anger because that's a prescriptive, one-size-fits-all solution that does not apply to every circumstance and may not be feasible. But what I can tell you is your anger is a beacon.

I discovered this when I had kids. They come to you as a tiny, helpless baby. And you know there will be crying, there will be sleepless nights, there will be so many things you can't possibly understand, and there will also be love. Parenting is great. Parenting is the best job in the world. You got this, Momma! You registered for a Boppy and a breast pump! You're on your way!

And everything goes fine for a while, maybe. And then comes one night when nothing you do will soothe this kid. All the tricks you've developed in the past seven weeks are garbage. This baby hates them, and apparently this baby hates you. Hates your guts. Hates your face. Hates your smell. Did you drink gasoline? That's what this breast milk tastes like, and this baby hates that too.

You put them in a bouncy seat on the washing machine. Screaming.

You carry them around your apartment in the special way they like: laying them across your forearm on their tummy, their legs dangling off each side. Screaming.

You walk around in a different way. Screaming.

You lay them down. Screaming. You drive around. Screaming.

You try to put the baby to sleep. What the hell is wrong with you? Are you stupid? It's 4:19 in the morning. This is screaming time, not sleeping time, bucko. You need to get with the program.

The closer you get to actual morning, the more panic sets in. Are we really gonna just not sleep? Is that the plan here? The baby keeps screaming and you start bargaining with God.

"God, I know this is probably way down your list today, but I know you have the power to make this kid stop screaming. Like, I know you could just make this go away. So can you do me a solid and just . . . help?"

And God does not hear your prayer or God is not interested in your prayer or God is busy with the trolling bro podcasters because the baby is still on one and you feel your soul dying while your lizard brain activates and there's only one thing for you to do and that is to join your baby in screaming. Why should your baby be the only one to get all this emotional abandon? And the screaming feels incredible because you are so mad: mad none of your tactics work; mad the trolling bro podcasters are taking all God's attention, even though you specifically asked for it; mad God isn't listening to you; mad at your baby; mad at your spouse sleeping soundly in your bedroom with the fancy sound machine because it is your night to be up and while you accept that, it's also like you couldn't come out like once to just check on us, even though in reality this would only piss you off more; mad you're going to get maybe two hours of sleep; just mad.

I'm mad because this is IMPORTANT TO ME. The books are all telling me sleep is crucial for the baby, the baby's brain cannot grow without sleep, the baby needs an insane amount of sleep to function, doesn't the baby know what the books say? And if her brain doesn't grow, she will never reach her developmental milestones, she'll make an 11 on her ACT, she'll never go to college—and on and on and on. And what about me? I know I am an absolute monster without sleep, so what about my brain, how will it grow without sleep? The amount of rage and frustration directly correlates to how important something is to me.

When we swallow that anger (whether it's at a baby who won't go the frick to sleep or an unjust system), we don't honor what anger is trying to indicate to us.

Your broken heart, your anger, your rage, your frustration, they're marquees naming what is important to you. And these will reveal everything you need to know about a person, about a group of people, about an institution, and about yourself. Allow the disturbance in your soul to be a compass pointing you in the direction of your next steps. It will help you see if you align with the people you thought you aligned with.

Your unsoothed heart is your most powerful weapon, and like our Lord and Savior Jesus Christ, we just have to know how to wield it.

What makes someone mad, what threatens their peace, what turns their world upside down is an indication of what they value. Applying this filter will help you understand if your anger (or any anger) is righteous or self-righteous.

As you consider your pressure points, maybe you need to know that the anger you hold against a religious institution is because you're not an idiot. You clearly see that 1 + 1 does not equal 3, even though everyone around you is saying it obviously does.

The anger you feel at the cognitive dissonance at the public witness of the people who taught you the Ten Commandments means you care.

The anger that broke your heart when you got kicked out of a faith community for asking questions is because that community meant something to you.

The anger that sits in your belly when you think about the way you participated in shutting someone out of youth group as a kid means you know you screwed up and it's a big deal.

Something I think gets lost in our anger is that anger begets action. Often, we begin in anger and end in despair, but if we look for the truth, we see that's not how Jesus dealt with his anger. Anger is not meant to sit in our chest; its place is not perpetually firing up our belly. All the smart thinkers tell us carrying it around is self-destructive, which I agree with. I posit that, like a dragon's fire, it needs to be breathed out into the world. But directed properly. Your anger is meant to stir you up so that you will do something about it. I believe our BIPOC sisters understand this better than White women do, echoing Maya Angelou's wise words: "Bitterness is like cancer. It eats upon the host. But anger is like fire. It burns it all clean."[1]

We fear anger for good reason: given free rein, it will absolutely kill you. Sit with it for too long and it coagulates into hate. Wielded irresponsibly, it will wound those who do not deserve it. Tranquilize it, and you'll numb yourself to death.

But if it's true what they say about us having Holy Spirit living inside us, could it be that there's a connection between what riles us up and what needs our sacred attention? The *Little Women* girlies know exactly what I'm talking about here, because this is perfectly exemplified in the character of Marmee.

I have Adult-Onset *Little Women* Fever from discovering the book and movies way into my grownhood via my dear friend Megan's guidance, so as a mom, I've always connected with Marmee. The mother of the aforementioned little women, Marmee, is kind, generous, and hard-working. She parents her daughters with intention and grace, and you never once see her lose her temper. Not when Amy burns Jo's novel, not when Jo almost unintentionally lets Amy drown, not even when Beth dies of scarlet fever. I remember reading Louisa May Alcott's dialogue from the scene after Amy falls through the ice while attempting to get back in Jo's good graces after setting fire to Jo's HANDWRITTEN NOVEL (I love Amy, but girl, you did us wrong). Amy nearly dies (okay, she doesn't deserve to drown for it), but once she's safe and warm, Marmee and Jo share a little heart-to-heart. Jo despairingly confesses to her mother that she's so angry, so deeply angry all the time, and that's what led to her trying to hurt Amy as Amy had hurt her.

Marmee makes a startling confession: "I am angry nearly every day of my life."[2]

In the book, Louisa May Alcott paints Marmee with the brush of perfection. She says, "I am angry nearly every day of my life, but I have learned not to show it; and I still try to hope not to feel it, though it may take me another forty years to do it."[3] Jo follows it up with a comment about how she hopes to follow in her mother's footsteps, snuggles into her, and the scene ends there.

Alcott grew up in a transcendentalist home and so I understand why she felt the need to make Marmee, who was modeled after her own mother, Abigail, have complete and total control over every aspect of her emotions, but there was no way I would ever come close to being a Marmee if this was how she handled her anger.

In 2019, Greta Gerwig gave us a new film version of *Little Women*, beautifully rendered and full of small tweaks and twists I believe Louisa would love, and if she doesn't, I don't want to talk about it. One of my favorites is during the anger conversation, when the actresses have this moment I've watched and read repeatedly.

But instead of "I have learned not to show it; and I still try to hope not to feel it" followed by Jo's hope she can do the same, in this version, Marmee looks Jo in the eye and says, "I hope you'll do a good deal better than me. There are some natures too noble to curb and too lofty to bend."[4] The best part about this dialogue change is that actress Laura Dern, who plays Marmee, found the line in a letter from Abigail Alcott to her daughter, Louisa May, during her research.[5] It's not that we need to hide our anger or train ourselves not to feel it, but by allowing ourselves to pay attention to it, we can understand so much about our priorities—if they are on the right level, and if we need a recalibration. It's not that Jo's anger was wrong, it's that it needed recalibration.

And I'm not talking about temper tantrums or hissy fits. I'm talking the holy rage that has you reaching for your Bible to make sure you're not wrong, Jesus did say we're supposed to love our enemies, right? This is the anger that bubbles up from your guts when you're trying to figure out why we're tithing for celebrity pastors to have a new Rolex when there are unhoused people two blocks away. The anger that will follow that thought almost immediately is that you yourself are no better than that celebrity pastor in your own special way.

Of course, this practice demands truth-telling with yourself because you can't assume all your anger is holy because you're so evolved spiritually. It's got to go through the filter of what made Jesus mad; otherwise, every jerk who cuts me off in traffic would be the recipient of some Spirit-led destruction courtesy of *moi*.

The key to anger is to keep moving through it. If you let it flow through you, it activates you to change. It's when you stuff it down and stop it up that you get yourself into trouble. So let your anger move you and keep moving through it— into agency, into action, into fighting for a world that can be better. Let the power team of your pissed-off, unsoothed heart and Holy Spirit point out what's important to you and let that guide you as you consider what's next for your little plot of land.

PUSHING
BOUNDARIES

Foraging in the Wilderness

My scientist friends have come up with things like "principles of uncertainty" and dark holes. They're willing to live inside imagined hypotheses and theories, but many religious folks insist on answers that are always true. We love closure, resolution, and clarity, while thinking that we are people of "faith"! How strange that the very word "faith" has come to mean its exact opposite.

Fr. Richard Rohr, *Universal Christ*

One very early November morning in Spain, my friend Elizabeth and I sat on a tour bus, breathing in exhaust fumes while a few older gentlemen shuffled past us to their seats. Our final cruise jaunt was to visit Santa Maria de Montserrat Abbey, outside the city of Barcelona. A few months earlier, I'd read the description of this excursion and knew immediately I had to do it, and Elizabeth, who is also nerdy about weird religious things, would be my sole companion. No one else on our trip would wake up at 6:45 a.m. to take a bus to a monastery in the mountains, but your girls were game.

179

As we sleepily wound our way through the waking streets of Barcelona and began the ascent, our guide hopped on the bus speaker to give us the history of the abbey and its most famous relic, La Moreneta, or the Black Madonna.

The legend goes that in 890 CE, a group of goatherds were tending their flocks in the Catalan mountains and became aware of a radiant light emanating from a cave above them. And because I imagine ninth-century goatherds are probably looking for ways to pass the time, when they saw a bright light up in the mountains, they decided to investigate.

As for me and my house, this sounds a lot like a great way to get killed or abducted by aliens. If there is a mysterious, otherworldly light of unknown origins, it seems the best thing to do is worry about my own self.

But the goatherds were not me, so they scrambled up the rock face, I assume leaving the me of the group behind to watch the goats and I guess let someone know when they died or were snatched up by God knows what. When they got there, inside the cave was a statue, a miracle, a marvel. A beautiful carved image of the Virgin Mary cradling the infant Christ, their skin dark and lovely with golden accents. The goatherds didn't dare touch her, the mother of Jesus holding her son, but they slid down the rock face back to the me of the group, who was *this close* to calling their moms. The goatherds ran to the people who would know what to do: the guys at the church in the town below. They told the religious authorities what they'd seen, and soon they were leading a bunch of old men the long way up to the cave. The light had dimmed, but when they arrived, she was still there, her gold crown and the sun's glow reflecting off baby Jesus's black toes.

As important religious men do, they had a meeting to decide what should be done next. The Madonna and her child belonged in a sacred space, that much was sure. The decision was made to take her down the mountain, enshrining her in a place better suited for her station. She belonged in the church, she belonged behind whatever the 890 CE version of velvet ropes and glass cabinetry was, she did not belong out here in the wild.

But the Black Madonna of Montserrat said, "Not today."

Legend says she simply refused to budge. One man attempted to remove her with brute strength. Another pulled out a tool to give him some leverage between the ground and the base of the statue, to no avail. One of the men took a rope from the goatherds and tried pulling. Nothing.

After months of trying to bring her down the mountain, it became clear the Black Madonna of Montserrat was going to stay exactly where she was found, thank you very much. If the people wanted to experience the miracle of the Black Madonna, they were going to have to leave what was comfortable and safe at the foot of the mountain. Sacred spaces, in the physical sense, were carefully boundaried, and to discover that the miraculous statue pushed against where God and God's work was or was not supposed to be was uneasy for some. Centuries of spiritual pilgrims have trekked up the mountain, encountering God in the wilderness along the way, just like the Black Madonna intended. It's almost as if she's saying, "Come see me, but take your time. I have things to show you along the way."

After you've set fire to the place you called home and you've cleared the land of both overgrowth and toxins in the soil, there comes a time when you will ask yourself, "What *do* I want to grow here?" And the only way to find out is to venture out from what you know into what you do not. The time will come to set out from your little plot of land to see what's growing out in the wilderness and decide what you want to bring home. I think of this process as pushing boundaries—exploring the edges to discover what might be flourishing there.

God isn't restrained by our attempts at theology any more than God is restrained by the walls of our churches. We endeavor to systemize this unknowable mystery with acronyms and charts and pamphlets, but these cannot begin to secure the wildness, the ferocity, the untamed tamer of chaos.

This is where it gets fun. And a little weird. Essentially, we're going foraging. But that requires leaving the places we know to discover what God might have for us beyond the boundaries we've always been comfortable within.

The best example I can give you is my own, when I decided to become the champion of Judas Iscariot, betrayer of Jesus Christ.

Even if you aren't a Christian, you probably get the gist about Judas: his name is synonymous with treachery. From the Scriptures, it's clear whoever is writing these Gospels, they hate Judas. They don't even let the narrative unfold for you; they are always reminding you Judas was a traitor and he sucks from the jump.

There is a series of portraits lining the lobby of my home church (she of mustard-gold carpet). These are portraits of the apostles, painted by legendary Panhandle artist Kenneth Wyatt. And look, he painted all the apostles White, okay? It's not great, we know that now. But these apostles in their frames always fascinated me. There is Peter, an old man with biceps to rival Antoni's from *Queer Eye*. There's Paul, a grump hunched amid candles as he wrote his letters to the churches all around the world. There's John with what I can only see as a Billy Ray Cyrus mullet. And at the end of the lobby, right before you leave, is Judas.

Judas is a scapegoat, and in art he's almost always portrayed as one. I'm not an art historian, but there are some patterns. He's consistently physically ugly, with shifty eyes and a hook nose (talk about racist stereotypes). If he's alive, he's kissing or about to kiss or just kissed Jesus. If he's dead, he's hanging from a tree, his thirty pieces of silver strewn on the ground. When you get to the medieval stuff, there's a devil pulling a demon baby out of his distended stomach, which I still have not uncovered the reasons for. In stained glass, he's often got a black halo, setting him apart from his once-friends, his likeness forever damned. And it's not just in visual art: when Dante wrote Judas into his *Inferno*, he placed the former apostle in the lowest circle of hell, head down inside the maw of Satan himself, where he's destined for all eternity to be chewed upon by one of Lucifer's three heads and have his back scratched by the devil's claws, which is not soothing or comforting like when your mom does it.

After reevaluating my origin story, after the lament, after asking the questions, I knew the work ahead of me was to understand exactly what I was claiming to believe. I needed to revisit the Gospels, the life of Jesus. I needed to detach myself from everything I'd ever been taught about Jesus and undergo the task of meeting him for myself. To see if the fuss was worth the fight. And doing my best to reread those gospel stories with the freshest eyes I could manage revealed a lot to me, but one stand-out revelation was that we have been real jerks to Judas.

Why was I suddenly feeling so much . . . *sympathy* for Judas in all his infamy? I couldn't quite put my finger on it, but I felt a certain resistance to instantly writing him off.

And as I'm reading, I'm also arguing with Religion Cop, who is real upset about me potentially catching feelings for this guy.

RELIGION COP

Snap out of it. He's smarmy and shady and shifty and he betrayed our Lord and Savior Jesus Christ, Erin. What is wrong with you? Do I need to write you up?

ERIN

Right, but he couldn't have been smarmy, shady, and shifty the entire time, right?

RELIGION COP

Are you making stuff up? About the Bible? Arrest her.

ERIN

Well, no, I mean, maybe, but the thing that sucks about history is it's written by whoever is left, and whoever was left really hated Judas.

RELIGION COP

Yeah, that is because he betrayed Jesus. I told you! We all told you! Everyone was right: this wilderness thing is bad news. You are headed down a bad road. Someone come and shame her before they accidentally send me to hell just for being around her. Pretty soon she'll start reading weird theology books or something.

Another light bulb moment for me during this foraging excursion was realizing one of my own boundaries, one I didn't even realize I had, was that I had only read old White Dutch male theologians and their American cheerleaders. Again, it's not that these guys are all bad (although some of them are!), it's that they were all I read. So not only was I missing out on a million rich theologies of thinkers and scholars of different races and genders and time periods, but I had inadvertently allowed that particular worldview to be the only one I was shaped by.

I had to remedy that, which lead to me reading lots of people, in particular Dr. Wilda Gafney, who introduced me to the concept of sacred imagination. Sacred imagination is the practice of thinking around and behind Scripture, using Holy Spirit as a guide for moving through narratives of Scripture to stay curious around the parts we're left to wonder about. It's not that you think these ideas you're imagining are canon, but they're interesting and birth new questions about stories you've read a million times.

And then Religion Cop says, *This sure sounds heretical.* Religion Cop is not a fan of sacred imagination.

But we press on because technically I'm out of his jurisdiction at this point, but I do have to keep reminding myself of that.

I started thinking about the years Judas must have spent with Jesus and the rest of the disciples, which I often envision as a sort of benevolent college fraternity, with jokes and arguments and stress and close quarter living arrangements. The smells were probably similar. But Judas saw all the things the future rock of the church, Peter, saw. He experienced the miracles, he healed people himself, and he heard the sermons. He had to know as much as any of the disciples knew, right?

And then there's the doctrine aspect of the Judas question. You can get really tied up in all the scholarly theories about free will and predestination that accompany the narrative around Judas's actions. Did he have a choice? Was he always going to betray Jesus? Did he do it out of a different ambition? Did Judas think he would kickstart the work Jesus was obviously here to do: freeing the Jews from Roman captivity? If he had a choice, what would the story be like if he didn't do it? Is he damned? Or did he repent?

Growing up not in the wilderness, the straightforward narrative was that Judas betrayed Jesus for thirty pieces of silver. The logical conclusion I drew as a child was he needed the money, but that didn't make any sense either because he was the Stacey McGill* of the disciples. Scripture even says he was already dipping into the coin purse (John 12:4–6).

So, what's the deal with Judas? Why was I so hung up on him? And why is Religion Cop still cruising around the block, watching to see when I'm going to step out of line?

Part of this pushing the boundaries and heading off into the wilderness is getting over the fear of being bad. You were a good kid, you stayed in the lines, you accepted what they wanted you to accept, but now you've got questions. There's a feeling in the back of your brain that you might stumble upon an idea or thought that will officially separate you from God, something so out of line, so bonkers God will be like, *That is too hot for me*. Part of our deprogramming includes realizing God is out here, too, past where the well-meaning and the control freaks have laid arbitrary perimeters. And exploration is not the same as pledging allegiance to a belief system. And belief systems are not the same as loving God.

I decided to lean into my curiosity. I kept digging into these Judas narratives. I read all the Apocrypha around Judas, listened to sermons, read commentary; I drank in anything I could find on the guy. Something bothered me about the idea that as a collective whole, we've given this guy a giant middle finger, painted a black halo over his head, and consigned him to eternal conscious torment in hell in the maw of Satan.

*Obviously, Stacey was the treasurer of The Baby-Sitters Club.

And here comes the cop again.

> **RELIGION COP**
> You know you're not God, right?

> **ERIN**
> Yeah, I know that.

> **RELIGION COP**
> And you understand that God's ways are not your ways? And God is so holy, so other, you can't possibly understand or comprehend his perfect nature, therefore while eternal conscious torment doesn't make sense to you, it's perfectly just for God. And if God wanted to use Judas as an object of wrath or a tool to bring about his own purposes, he can do whatever he damn well pleases, and not answer to you or your inflated sense of morality.

> **ERIN**
> I understand that is a way you could look at it.

> **RELIGION COP**
> Okay, but that's the way we've always looked at it, so why are you changing now?

> **ERIN**
> I'm really just, like, adventuring. I don't know if I'm changing. I'm just browsing, I guess?

> **RELIGION COP**
> Hope you don't die during this adventure. Seems risky and a good way to end up being eternally, consciously tormented.

Religion Cop sucks. He needs to be reminded that this is not really his precinct anymore.

So we forage. We discover a fruit, maybe something like liberation theology, which is a way to understand God's work to free humanity from slavery, both physically and spiritually. When we take a bite, maybe we find a seed called redemptive hell, the idea that sin has consequences, but God does not punish us eternally; rather, God will always give us a way to repent and return.

Maybe in our exploration we discover a very weird and interesting looking plant growing out here—it looks like something called universal salvation, that God desires everyone to come to God (before you trip, it's familiar to you because Paul wrote about it in his letters: peep Romans 5:18, 1 Corinthians 15:22, and Romans 11:32 for starters).

Maybe you find a flower, one that grew on your land before, a pure, simple statement of God's love: that God so loved this world, that he sent his Son, that whoever simply believes in that Son will not die, but will enjoy eternal life, kiss or no kiss. It goes in the foraging basket. You want to plant that one again.

What bugs me about the Judas narrative I grew up with is the suggestion that someone—and by extension, any of us—can go beyond God's grace. When I use my sacred imagination, I am Judas. I can put myself in the sandals of a man who really loved Jesus, who was slightly (or really) impatient, and who really wanted events to move in a way he thought they should. I have been the idiot who watched in horror as events I put into motion spiraled outside of my control to a devastating end. I have absolutely done the wrong thing. Made a huge mistake. Blown it in a momentous way. I can place myself within the hopelessness of a man who experienced isolation from his dearest brothers and sisters, his chosen family for the past three years. A man who made a profound error in judgment, who was alone, and who could not possibly see what would happen if he just held on a little longer. When Judas ceases to be a prop in the story, he becomes human. And when he's human, we have a lot more in common than we often acknowledge. And I cannot help but see myself in him.

And if I see myself in him, I don't want to write him off. If Judas is a proxy for me, for any of us, I don't want to brush him aside and throw him in hell with no hope for redemption. I want to believe for him, so I can believe for myself, that there is no condemnation for those who are in Jesus. I want to know for him, so I can know for myself, that nothing, neither angels nor demons, life nor death, nothing can separate us from the love of Christ. Because if it's not real for him, it's not real for me. If it's not good news for him, it's not for me.

Is Judas outside of God's grace? I don't know his inner life. I can't definitively state his motivations and intentions, I can only guess. But humanizing Judas became an icon of my struggle with how we demonize questions and doubts, how we engage our imaginations and minds with our faith, how we vilify the wilderness by making even thinking about things in a new way heretical.

I tentatively brought this up to my spiritual director, nervous she would kick me off her roster. She didn't and encouraged me to do some imaginative prayer (Religion Cop says, *Jezebel!*). As we talked through the prayer, we ended up at the Harrowing of Hell.

The Harrowing of Hell is the most badass extrabiblical event, but we have no idea if it actually happened. It's one of the first examples of Christian sacred imagination, and although we get allusions to it in places like 1 Peter 4:6 and

Ephesians 4:9, the fullness of this story is best laid out in an apocryphal work called The Gospel of Nicodemus, which got super popular during the medieval ages. The basic gist is this: between his death and resurrection, Jesus was busting down the gates of hell and pulling out everyone who had died before his atonement was complete. It was a big motif in early Christian art; you've probably seen it but never noticed it before. There's Jesus, usually with Adam and Eve, pulling them out of their coffins by their wrists, and getting them the hell out of hell.

But as my spiritual director and I prayed, I visualized searching this particular bowel of hell for others. (Does everyone else's imaginative prayer take them to hell or just mine?) Who else was down there? A small coffin, new, just there a few hours. Jesus walks over and nudges the lid off, revealing the surprised face of one of his dearest friends. Jesus reaches down, grabs Judas's wrist, and pulls him out.

I cry every time I think about it.

If you've ever attempted to break out of a preprogrammed pattern of thinking, if you've ever tried to bust through a shame cycle, you know what comes after something like this. Oh, look. He's back.

RELIGION COP

You have lost your mind. Jesus taking Judas to heaven? First of all, the theological implications of this are off-the-charts problematic. Not to mention that again, we're just making stuff up to, I guess, feel good? Under whose authority are you making these claims? Who gave you the right? You don't have the qualifications, the intelligence, the moral compass, the understanding, or the faith, apparently, to bring any kind of illumination to these texts and what they might mean to our lives now. Just be quiet, accept the teachings as they were told to you, and quit all of this. You're talking about a God I don't even recognize.

And to Religion Cop, I just want to say: that is the point. You're talking about a God I don't recognize either. Why do you get to be the arbiter of who God is and who God is not? Who says you're the gatekeeper of truth, just because you happen to be loud? Who gave you the final authority on interpretations? If I don't have it, then maybe you don't either, and maybe we should cut each other some slack.

Pushing these boundaries and foraging for new things to grow, following the Black Madonna into the cliffs of Montserrat or Jesus redeeming Judas Iscariot, gave me an understanding of how small and irrelevant God was to me previously. Powered by what Fr. Richard Rohr calls "practical atheism,"[1] which just means sure, I say I believe in Jesus, but it doesn't really affect any part of my life—I make my own way. I've also made God in my own image, which means I never have to be confronted or challenged by new information or interpretations or experiences. The reason I needed to set fire to my little plot of land to begin with was simply because this God was absolutely not one worth knowing in the long run.

And that is what the life of faith is: the long run. No onetime transactions. No final exams. No trophies or award shows. You're not walking down the aisle to accept Jesus Christ as your personal Lord and Savior; he's raising you from the dead. You yourself are not a rigid inventory of theological beliefs, you're in a cosmic conversation with Divine Love and the rest of the universe: "He was supreme in the beginning and—leading the resurrection parade—he is supreme in the end. . . . So spacious is he, so expansive, that everything of God finds its proper place in him without crowding. Not only that, but all the broken and dislocated pieces of the universe—people and things, animals and atoms—get properly fixed and fit together in vibrant harmonies, all because of his death. . . . The mystery in a nutshell is just this: Christ is in you, so therefore you can look forward to sharing in God's glory" (Col. 1:18–20, 26–29).

We've squeezed and forced our connection with God into a panini press, hissing out our list of doctrinal bullet points so everyone knows where we stand and what that means for who is in and who is out. We've put a fence around God, to the point that we get offended if we consider that a God who it's said is so rich in mercy—because of the great love God has for us, that even when we were already dead, this God made us alive again—could possibly forgive the man who betrayed him.

But the harder I push on the boundaries, the more I learn the ways people of the past have processed God in their own ways, the less I pay attention to Religion Cop in my head and the more I explore, the more comfortable I become with befriending mystery. The more I wonder if my relationship with God, our connection, my faith, this cosmic conversation, is less a way to be definitive about a theological belief and more of an invitation to trust and be with the presence of love that goes deeper than I will ever know.

Is there a story here amid the weight of truth that looks like hope? And is it enough hope to build my life around? Am I willing to risk God being bigger than I can understand, small enough to be cozy in an atom, defying neat stacks of dogma, alive in everything and outside of everything? Can my heart and brain manage to exist in a world where that God is humming within every person's humanity and sometimes, they cut me off in traffic? Can I see God in the Black Madonna in the Catalan mountains and at the DMV?

The more I study Scripture, the more aware I am of the history of interpreting Scripture and how we got it and where we found it and the translation processes, the more I am convinced that Scripture is an invitation to conversation, not a way to be definitive. There are things we can know, and there are things nebulous. Am I okay with that? Can I make a place for myself within the vast library of varied ways ancient peoples made sense of God? Again, is there a story in here that looks like hope? And is it enough hope for me to build my life around?

When you first begin to befriend mystery, it's nerve-racking, because mystery is so unpredictable and, well, mysterious. Before you came out into the wilderness, you pretty much knew how God worked. At least you thought you did. You knew who was in and who was out. You knew how experiences with God were going to go. Scripture held no questions because everything was anticipated. But befriending mystery is not just accepting that you might not know some things. It's free-falling into trust. It's relaxing into uncertainty (I get hives about it too, it's okay). It's not a perfect relationship, but you can be at ease with each other.

When I expand the boundaries of my understanding of God, knowing it pushes past my own comprehension, it helps me realize all the things I cannot possibly know. All the questions I have that cannot be answered, instead of being stumbling blocks, they become connection points. Krista Tippett says it this way: "In life, in religion, in science, this I believe: any conviction worth its salt has chosen to cohabit with a piece of mystery, and that mystery is at the essence of the vitality and the growth of the thing."[2] When I'm not forcing an infinite God into a systematic theology textbook, I am free to see God as love and people as beloveds instead of conversion projects or the enemy. When I let go of making an idol of God in my own image, it challenges me to be more loving, more compassionate, more committed to honoring the Jesus I see in everyone, as opposed to wanting to be right and correct and superior. I am not bound by my own understanding and my own guardrails. There's always so much more. The wilderness has shown me this more than anything else.

We can know a lot of things: we can know what Athanasius said at this council or why Arius got kicked out of this one. We can know Scripture front and back. We can have a history of following God, of being a good Christian, of having faith in hard times. We can be a pillar of our church; we can be blessed with gifts that honor and encourage the body of Christ. We can know our list of theological imperatives and quote them from memory. Befriending mystery doesn't mean we can't have knowledge, doesn't mean we can't have standards, doesn't mean we can't have wisdom or practice discernment.

Some things will always baffle us. Some things, like the Black Madonna showed us, don't want to be found in typical places. They only show up in the wilderness. Sometimes the clouds part and there is understanding and it is not an answer we want. In the pushing of the boundaries, in the places where we exchange tight-fisted certainty for open-handed trust, there is yet another invitation. One we should seriously consider RSVPing to, according to the apostle Paul in his first letter to the church in Corinth:

> Love never dies. Inspired speech will be over some day; praying in tongues will end; understanding will reach its limit. We know only a portion of the truth, and what we say about God is always incomplete. But when the Complete arrives, our incompletes will be canceled. . . . We don't yet see things

clearly. We're squinting in a fog, peering through a mist. But it won't be long before the weather clears and the sun shines bright! We'll see it all then, see it all as clearly as God sees us, knowing him directly just as he knows us! (1 Cor. 13:8–10, 12)

Paul with the truth-telling and hope-having.

When you live in the wilderness, you might need to trade being right for a new, more relaxed way to live. Befriending mystery comes with the side effect of not feeling compelled to make sure everyone knows you don't agree with how they live or what they believe. You may experience fatigue when doing things you once loved, like engaging in quiet self-righteousness, or getting your panties in a wad about gatekeeping God so that God stays put. Paul, at the end of his chapter about love, has a helpful suggestion. He says until we don't have to peer through the mist, until the fog lifts, until the mystery is revealed, "until that completeness, we have three things to do to lead us toward that consummation: Trust steadily in God, hope unswervingly, love extravagantly. And the best of the three is love" (1 Cor. 13:13). There it is. That's the work we have to do.

Turn over that foraging basket. Let's see what you've got in there, because now that we've cleared out the invasive species and toxins in the soil, we've got some planting to do. And I don't know about you, but I'm ready to see some good things grow.

MAKING
PEACE

But What If You're Wrong?

> Everybody is wrong about everything, just about all the time.
>
> Chuck Klosterman, *Sex, Drugs, and Cocoa Puffs*

What God and I frequently argue about is that God is not taking my suggestions for who is on the list and who the bouncer turns away at the door. Yes, she who is dancing the cosmic dance with the mystery of Divine Love is still such a butthead.

I feel as though I've compiled a pretty decent list of standards people who claim to follow God should be about, but God keeps telling me, "Thanks, but I think I've got it." Or as Barbara Brown Taylor says:

> I'm not in charge of this House, and never will be. I have no say about who is in and who is out. I do not get to make the rules. . . . I am a guest here, charged with serving other guests—even those who present themselves as my enemies. I am allowed to resist them, but as long as I trust in one God who made us all, I cannot act as if they are no kin to me.

There is only one House. Human beings will either learn to live in it together or we will not survive to hear its sigh of relief when our numbered days are done.[1]

If you're reading this, you don't need me to tell you how quick our faith tradition is to vilify someone or a group of someones who we deem are "wrong."

If you believe this, you're wrong. You've capitulated to the world.

I'll be honest, I have some thoughts about this. In my opinion, a lot of my siblings in Christ act like dang fools frequently and with great vigor. I believe they care about the wrong things. I believe they vote the wrong ways. I believe they pervert the gospel with aplomb. I believe they don't read the same Bible I do, or, at the very least, their interpretation button is broken. I wish we could relegate some of these family members to "weird cousin" status. Put them in the back of the family photo. Maybe accidentally give them the wrong dates for the family reunion. Oops. Our bad.

And what really chaps my hide is their self-righteous obstinacy that their understanding is THE only God-approved version there ever was, and they are the only ones who understand exactly what God meant, therefore everyone else is not only an idiot, they are a heretic and definitely going to hell, unless they repent the way they think they should, and that's, as the kids say, on God.

The only problem is, "they" could say the exact thing about me.

So, who's right and who's wrong? If we're really going to put stock in this whole "it's a mystery" business, then why are we getting so hot and bothered when we feel the family going rogue? Or maybe we're the ones going rogue. How can any of us be so *sure*?

Of all the things I miss postdeconstruction, I long for my old friend Blessed Assurance the most.

We had good times together. Standing resolutely around a flagpole in junior high, convinced we were taking back this godless school system for the Lord. Walking my freshman biology class through a young Earth version of creation (Ah! Youth!) the day after we learned about evolution. Highlighting almost all of *The Christian Hedonist* by John Piper and casually dropping quotes into conversation with the Reformed boy I thought was cute. Having an answer for everything. Smugly weaponizing Scripture. Being confident I absolutely understood everything in its original intent, never curious, always sure that my interpretation (or at least the interpretation of the people I listened to) was correct and unimpeachable.

But we had to break up, me and my old friend Blessed Assurance, because after years of trying to doll up assurance so it looked like faith, I realized the two were not compatible. And when you give up on Blessed Assurance, there's one question on the lips of everyone still huddled around the flagpole:

But what if you're wrong?

Some days I think the old adage attributed to St. Augustine is possible: "In essentials, unity; in non-essentials, liberty; in all things; charity."* I believe in the one holy, catholic, and apostolic church. I believe we can keep the main thing the main thing. The thing that matters most does not have to be at the mercy of the thing that matters the least.

Some days I am adamantly convinced to believe such a thing is foolish. I am an optimist; I am a hope-quester or

*Well, we think he said it. It might also have been German theologian Rupertus Meldenius, but this one is kind of an "in conclusion, no one knows."

whatever we're calling the opposite of a doomscroller. But I know we cannot even agree on what love looks like or on the definition of unity. I know we are all scared of the same things that take a million different forms, so we all fight our battles with distinct methods. We call each other "divisive" because while we know our God has called us to unity, we believe the other side is making unforgivable transgressions, and we cannot be unified with that.

Everyone has a line, and even the man we all claim to follow had a line, though our lives and priorities look different.

And from what I can tell, the line he consistently wasn't willing to cross was dehumanization.

He called the religious leaders of the day "snakes" for imposing frivolous rules and rituals on the people, overburdening them for no good reason and keeping them busy with hair-splitting. He returned dignity to those who were considered unclean and unfit—the bleeding woman, lepers, and people with demons—allowing them back into society to flourish and live in community. As he died, he remembered his mother would have no one to care for her after he was gone, so he gave charge of her to one of his dearest friends, ensuring that each of them would be a comfort to the other in the hard days to come. He loved people back into their humanity, back into their belovedness as children of God.

A mystical process takes place when you begin to know you are loved as Jesus loves you. It's always available to you, but to receive it you have to accept the invitation to allow yourself to be loved. And that means being vulnerable.

You risk looking like an idiot. You risk the potential for heartbreak. You take a chance on lowering your defenses and allowing yourself to be loved as a child of God instead of adhering to a belief system where you know all the answers. It's the difference between reading the menu on your phone and tasting the first bite in a fine-dining experience. It's the difference between knowing your Bible trivia and dancing with Divine Love.

My brothers and sisters, the secret we're all hiding in our hearts but are too afraid to say out loud is that we all know we must be wrong. At least about some of it. We posture and preen, saying, "The Bible is extremely clear," to hide the fear that we've hitched our wagon to the wrong horse. We push our agendas as forcefully as possible to distract from the notion of what not being correct could mean. We are so afraid to be free. We, like the religious leaders of Jesus's day, build obstacle courses and hedge mazes around our hearts to make the greatest commandment a checklist we can mark off instead of a way of life to embody. We trade loving God with knowing about God and end up flat on our faces in both efforts.

There might be lots of reasons for this, but one I've uncovered is a core belief from those early days, something I really didn't pick up from one source as much as it was in the evangelical water and seeped into everything: just what an absolute degenerate sinner I am, and how God can barely tolerate my presence.

Jesus has to stand in front of me in heaven so God's wrath doesn't blow my protons and neutrons straight into hell. Yes, Jesus saved me, but gah, it was a close one.

So, you might say our generalized anxiety about who's in, who's out, and ultimately who's right makes sense. Of course, we're terrified of getting it wrong, and equally terrified of letting this fear show, and that's complex to live with. Because if we're wrong, then we're out.

Jesus himself said that the primary invitations are to love God and love your neighbor as yourself, but there can be no room for loving your neighbor as yourself if you actually hate yourself, if you truly believe that God resentfully puts up with you, but only if you get your ish together.

Especially for those of us who grew up in evangelical culture, we were taught to distrust ourselves, to see ourselves first and foremost as sinners, disobedient little rat finks, filled to the brim with selfishness and hate and idolatry. I'm not necessarily saying we aren't influenced by these things, but I would not say the same emphasis was put on our belovedness as children of God. Because we are certainly that as well, and let's get real, we were beloved *first*. When we get it twisted and believe our deepest identity is as sinners, our sin and the things that separate us from God end up becoming greater than how we are treasured, we are held, we are cherished and adored.

When we believe maybe God loves us but doesn't like us all that much unless we behave ourselves, we start believing that God hates the things we do, God hates when we mess up, God is disappointed by every step out of line. We become a child constantly berated for every mistake, certain we are a burden, constantly reabsorbing our own forsakenness, and assuming what we do is who we are. We look around every corner for punishment, bracing ourselves for the next blow.

If we want the good fruit, and not the invasive weeds, to grow on our little plot of land, Jesus asks us to do many difficult things in the name of love: to love our enemies, to love our neighbors as ourselves, to love the least of these—the people on the fringes who get ignored. So these are the seeds we must sow. And it's obvious Jesus wants us to push that love outside of our own experience. But the Swiss psychiatrist Carl Jung offers a perspective that might ride in tandem:

> That I feed the hungry, that I forgive an insult, that I love my enemy in the name of Christ—all these are undoubtedly

great virtues. What I do unto the least of my brethren, that I do unto Christ. But what if I should discover that the least among them all, the poorest of all the beggars, the most impudent of all the offenders, the very enemy himself—that these are within me, and that I myself stand in need of the alms of my own kindness—that I myself am the enemy who must be loved—what then?[2]

Using our sanctified common sense here, we know Jesus isn't asking us to love ourselves in a way that the world sees love, but with his love. With a love that stands firm in our identity as beloved.

May I posit that many of us truly have not understood the implications of our belovedness? We are not fully able to see the belovedness of anyone else because we still believe, deep down, we are unworthy of love. Until we open ourselves to the possibility of God loving us, yes, and liking us, enjoying us, we will not be able to believe it's true for anyone else. Jesus doesn't have to psych himself up to suffer through an encounter with you. God doesn't tolerate you, rolling their eyes at Holy Spirit behind your back. Jesus isn't sitting at a desk like an IRS auditor, peering at you over his readers and listing out all the ways you screwed up and all the ways he cannot wait to gleefully punish you for your transgressions.

Until we can imagine Jesus lying on a bean bag at a sleepover, eyes closed as every girl plays the song that's most meaningful to them, we will not see that we are liked and loved.

Until we can picture God bringing a labored-over side dish to the barbeque, we will not understand that we are liked and loved.

Until we can visualize God in a place where we're certain God would not go because those people could not be liked or loved, we will not comprehend our own soul-deep likability and innately lovable belovedness. We will not know peace.

I'll level with you. When you really break it down to brass tacks, when you weigh the evidence, just based on data, believing in God is not a smart move. There are times when I'm scrolling on Instagram and someone's made a cute little Richard Dawkins quote graphic that says something like: "Faith is the great cop-out, the great excuse to evade the need to think and evaluate evidence. Faith is the belief in spite of, even perhaps because of, the lack of evidence,"* and I'm like . . . well, points were made.

So what if we not only have our theology wrong, we're wrong about God, about Jesus, about all of it? If we're just carbon-based life-forms floating in a void of nothingness, with no point to existence, then what will we spend our one precious life doing? Who will we be? Because the truth is, we can't know intellectually or rationally that God exists. No one can prove God. We can make our best guesses, even educated guesses. But we certainly cannot analytically, 100 percent say our particular brand of God is the right one. I've had what I consider experiences with God. I've sat on the rim of Palo Duro Canyon with all my friends as the sun came up, bursting into purples and pinks and oranges, and felt transcendence. I've had a dream where my grandfather and I were building a house together that I believe I'll see again someday. I have stared for a straight hour into the eyes of my baby, knowing I am in her and she is in me, and we are

---

*I don't actually know if Dawkins said this, and as we know, Instagram is rife with misattribution, so keep your head on a swivel.

bound together in some miraculous way that exists outside of the physical world. I have known the love of God in all the ways I believe God sends God's love to me.

I believe in God, but my belief does not make God so.

Cards on the table: it's not my desire that you close this book and decide it's time for you to sever your connection with God. I know that will be the natural path some take after a season of deconstruction, and I understand that. But my landing brought me here: I can't be certain of who or what God is, but I better be damn sure whatever I land on will be worth giving up my life for. That's why I can't waste my time on tiny God in a box of my own making. It's already proven its worthlessness. Too-tiny theology is a deadly jungle of toxins and invasive species that gatekeeps, hoards, and ultimately kills. I have to divorce myself from tiny God in a box of my own making. Because if I believe in God, what I believe about God says everything about the kind of world I believe God is making, and that matters right now.

So, no, we don't want to be wrong. It's embarrassing, it's uncomfortable, and there's too much at stake.

But of course, we're all at least a little bit wrong about God, simply because we're *not* God. If you're right about God, exactly right about everything around God, that makes you God. And you are lovely, remember? Deeply likable and innately beloved. But not God.

So what in the world are we supposed to do in this quandary of high stakes and limited knowledge?

I think we stick to the basics the best we can.

Not one of us is an expert, and no amount of apologetics or education or Blessed Assurance will change the fact that we do not know everything and at the very least, we're all probably wrong about everything 80 percent of the time. I think this might be why Jesus helpfully was like, *Would you like for me to sum up the whole law for you in two bullet points? Love the Lord your God with all your heart, soul, and mind and love your neighbor as yourself.*

What if that was it?

What if loving God and loving people is the work of our lives, and we filter everything in our faith through that?

Imagine it were so. Would that, could that possibly offer you peace? Real, honest peace? Not to erase your questions or your grief or what you've lived through, but a way to plant them?

Did you know there are certain types of seeds tucked away in conifers, sealed with cement-hard resins that cause them to lay dormant for decades? No amount of sun, water, or good soil can crack the cone and cause the seed to germinate.

The only thing that releases the seed is fire.

Maybe it needs the fire to melt the resin or a chemical reaction from smoke and plant matter, but nothing other than fire will liberate that seed.

If we were able to make peace with what vexes us, to be tender with our origins, to honor our grief, we might find the charred pine cones of our past are cracking open, burrowing into our unpolluted soil, and maturing into shade trees, where there is peace among the wild things growing here.

What if we released ourselves from being right or being first or being on top or smartest and we simply tried to focus on these two things: love the Lord your God with all your heart, soul, and mind and love your neighbor as yourself? I think we'd have enough of a challenge to keep our hands full. We'd have enough interpretations of what that looks like to work on that for a good while. What if Jesus really meant it when he said that was it?

Even if we are carbon-based life-forms, floating around in a void of nothingness with no soul, and our death means only food for worms, to me, orienting my life around a God who insists in the same breath that we love people while we're loving God is worth it. Everything else is secondary. Even if it's not real, that would be a worthy mark to leave here. If the God I worshiped was a God of love, a God who left a final word of love and asked God's people to worship through loving others, I could waste my life on that.

Would it be worth the struggle to fight to see the humanity of the people who actively work against the flourishing of others? Would it be worth doing everything in my power to try and make vulnerable souls (non-souls, whatever) feel safe on this planet? Would it be worth it to snuggle my kids and plant a garden with my husband and drink wine with my family and sit in communal silence with my grandmother and lay flowers on graves and sing in church and walk with friends and read books and watch sunsets and thank God for all of it?

Yes. I think it would.

If we can't be sure, I'd rather risk my life on the belief that God is love. I'd rather plant that flag in the sand. That can be my banner. Not because of heaven or hell. But because the love Jesus espouses is worth the gamble of being wrong. And I'm going to be wrong about some of it. So where should I err?

And would it be enough for me to accept that, like everyone else who has ever graced the surface of this planet, I am a beloved child of this God of love? And that simple yet transcendent truth might rip through any notion I had about being right or wrong or better or worse and allow me to live with a heart attuned to the hopes of others and the presence of God? Is this what he meant by "my yoke is easy, and my burden is light"?

Could it really be that simple?

Could we really be that delusional?

Could that offer peace in all our tension?

At some point, we are tasked with braving a deconstruction of our deconstruction. Was the Hobby Lobby sign hanging in the church bathroom saying "Let Go and Let God" actually right? Is it the honest truth baptized in hope that believing we are loved and working to see it's true for everyone is the task of our lives?

In my college church experience, there was a big push for us to "leave room for mystery" when it came to God. What that really referred to was all the things we didn't have answers wrapped neatly in a bow for, but you needed to be able to quickly articulate everything else. Mystery was really just a small piece of the pie. "Leave room for mystery," we'd say while learning exactly how to defeat any atheist who would ever want to debate us about the existence of God (I've been alive for forty-one years and no atheist has ever wanted to debate me).

But of course, it's the reverse; we had it upside down all along. The pie chart of the things we know is a sliver, and the mystery makes up the majority. What we have to go on is an ancient library of books written over the course of centuries, translated imperfectly, and interpreted—with mostly good intentions—out of personal bias.

What we have is our own spiritual experience, understood in the best ways we know how with the humble tools we possess.

What we have is rainbow eucalyptus, breastfeeding, Fermi bubbles.

What we have is the miracle of friendship, recognizing someone you love by their footsteps, laughing until you pee your pants, strangers making sure strangers have something to eat, the physical feeling of a breaking heart, the communal effervescence of belting a beloved song at a concert.

Do carbon-based life-forms floating in a void of nothingness grab their chests and dramatically fall off the couch when Mr. Darcy finally tells Elizabeth he loves her?

Do bipedal mammals who supposedly have no souls stand in front of Michaelangelo's *Pietà* and weep?

Do highly evolved primates floating through life toward their inevitable blank space forgive? Do they feel God in the wind? Do they have memories? Do they love?

I have my hunches.

Of course, we limited humans are going to get some things wrong about God. But does a God concerned with theological preciseness let an on-the-run enslaved girl in a patriarchal society be the first human to give God a name?

If Jesus was so worried about everyone conforming to the exact same beliefs, why didn't he spend more time in the temples, clarifying Scripture with the rabbis, instead of hanging out with kids and telling stories?

Why would a God hellbent on handing out retaliatory measures of punishment roam around Palestine healing people?

When a rich man asked him what he must do to have eternal life, why didn't Jesus map out the five points of Calvinism?

Does a God troubled with getting every answer perfect send his Word in the form of a God-man who he allows to be interpreted by flawed humans over the course of two thousand years in a library of sometimes confusing and opposing essays instead of sending an angel with a systematic theology textbook?

We're not planting fields of flawless and unerring knowledge. We tried that, and when we attempted to be people alongside that fruit, we starved. It didn't have any nutritional value.

Of course we're wrong. Could it be that getting it right was never the goal in the first place?

Our curiosity is good. Our doubts are appropriate. Our questions are legitimate. The fact that we won't get off this planet with all questions answered is not an easy pill to swallow. The truth that we can't be right is hard, but it's also an invitation to a party you're already dancing at: trust. In all the ways we think we're in control, the honest truth is that we're not. We can fight it, or we can trust an imperfect path to a God of love and show our wobbly, shaky-kneed love to that God by loving every other messed-up carbon-based life-form as ourselves.

Not one minute or inch or iota of this is easy, and we will often fail miserably. We will forget who we are and who the God we've chosen to commit ourselves to is, all because the traffic was bad, or someone forgot to thaw the meat. The diagnosis will be terminal, the election won't go our way, the world will push back, the loss will come too soon. I lost my ever-loving mind the other day because someone keeps taking one of my socks from the sock burger and leaving the spare. It will be a good thing we've committed ourselves to love above all other charters because here is where it will need to be applied liberally.

Alexander Pope once mused, "To err is human." We've taken the Book of our spiritual ancestors and held it up as a template to copy when I think it's meant as a beacon in the night. Pages and pages and story after story of humans trying to figure out what God wants from them, how to reconcile a record of their heritage with the understanding of their belovedness. A continuous call-and-response:

"Do you love us?"

"Yes, I love you."

"Show us you love us."

"Open your eyes, I'm trying."

For a tribal people in ancient Mesopotamian culture, that beloved call-and-response looked like a God who escorted them from being enslaved foreigners to becoming a powerful and established kingdom. It took the form of a God who would perform miracles to release them, push back waters to set them free, offer forgiveness when they were seduced by other gods.

For a people conquered and falling from grace, it looked like attempting to narrate the story of their captivity in a way that walked them back into redemption after the unthinkable happened.

For first-century Roman outposts in the Middle East, that looked like following customary laws in enemy-occupied territory while waiting for deliverance. It meant doing the best they could with what they had and adhering to the rituals of their people.

For the disciples, it meant fumbling and grasping at straws while trying to keep up. Getting sent on missions to heal, seeing miracles performed before their eyes, watching dead men walk, and walking in friendship with a man who they sometimes think is the Son of God, maybe. That even when he told them clearly, they still didn't understand. Even after he left, they still couldn't figure out how any of it was supposed to work.

For us, it looks like sorting through two thousand years of misinterpretation and bias and state-sponsored propaganda and our own religious trauma.

Let us no longer pretend we've got it all figured out. Let us admit we're all grasping in the dark, and the more loving choice is to lay down our swords instead of sharply wielding them. Wielding a sword in broad daylight already takes a good amount of skill so as not to hurt you or anyone else. If you slash and stab and cut in the dark, you are bound to draw blood in the name of something you might be wrong about.

Is the wound worth it? Is it ever?

What if the fact that we don't get all the answers, but we do get the directive to love, is the ultimate task of Heracles? What if our job really is to love people, in all their impossibilities, with all their untidy lines and uncomfortable beliefs and inconvenient circumstances? Their distasteful perspectives, their fear-based jerk-holery, and all the dumb ways they manage to not see things the ways we want them to?

What if our job is to try with everything in us to see each other as God sees us, the truth of who we are, with the hope that this love, unbound by qualifications and regulations, will actually bring us further into the truth of ourselves? When we can free ourselves from a dogmatic assertiveness around every single belief we hold, those love muscles get flexed. We stop seeing our neighbors as sparring partners and watch with fresh eyes as they transform into God's children, who are longing for safety, hungering for care, and being extremely awkward (or even destructive) in their quest for it.

Just like us.

I am absolutely not advocating for inserting yourself into an unsafe or unhealthy relationship or institution. Sometimes the most loving thing we can do is remove ourselves from a toxic environment or a person's toxic behavior and allow them to go their own way. That is for your therapist, Holy Spirit, and you to work out.

With that said, it's easy to have opinions about what happens during the Eucharist or whether women should be able to preach. We can sort through the Koine Greek of Paul's letters and study first-century Roman culture to decide what he meant when he wrote this particular word and what that means for church hierarchy. It takes almost no emotional labor to intellectualize the process of sanctification and justification.

What will cost you everything, what you will need to lay down your life for, what will actively break your heart every single day, is love. Whether it takes the form of helping a refugee family get settled in a new place, tenderly caring for your aging mother-in-law in your own retirement, taking a trauma course in order to better connect with your people, always showing up with a baked good that reminds people you're thinking of them, managing a neighborhood pool with kindness and less annoyance than you have every right to have, sensing when a friend is down and reaching out to remind them of their belovedness, joking that you are ambivalent about kids but showing up to protest gun violence in schools, making treasure hunts for your nieces and nephews who secretly kind of drive you crazy, working diligently to serve foster families, driving all night to rescue your son from a terrible living situation, forgiving your partner when it would be easier to hold a grudge, whipping up that egg salad that one lady likes so much, writing to your congressperson, not forgetting, not ignoring, staying, watching, waiting, actively choosing not to dehumanize no matter what. There are a million ways to be the love of God.

We're all carrying around a fear that we're wrong, that we'll get found out, that the armor we've carefully soldered for safety purposes will crack, and we'll be exposed. And all this is much harder to practice off the pages of a book when not everyone is as committed to the visions of collective love as you are. But when you make space for the vulnerability of being comfortable in love, instead of standing in what you hope and pray is your rightness, you might be surprised who finds relief in you. You might be surprised when peace settles into your soil. You might be surprised what happens when love spreads over everything, settling into the cracks and crevices of who you are, and you begin to understand what John meant when he said, "Perfect love drives out fear" (1 John 4:18 NIV).

Are you able to perfectly love anything or anyone? No— again, you're not God here. But in the attempt, you'll discover you don't have to be afraid of working out faith, of being a person, of trying and failing, of risking your whole life on something as deranged as being right about Love.

REBUILDING AND REWILDING

How Does Your Garden Grow?

The fruit of the Spirit . . . gives a sure sign of transformed character. When our deepest attitudes and dispositions are those of Jesus, it is because we have learned to let the Spirit foster his life in us.

Dallas Willard, *The Great Omission*

Everything is a choice, right? You get to choose if you'll worship a God who liberates or one who imprisons. You get to choose if you'll serve the disconnection of adamantly proclaiming your rightness or connection in your wrongness.

You get to choose what gets planted on this freshly revitalized little plot of land. You get to choose what goes, what stays, and what to let rewild. Because just as your body knows how to heal, so does the land, and rewilding is the process of letting the land *heal*. At its utmost, rewilding is simply the natural process of conservation.

Paul says it like this: "Do you not know that as many as were baptized into Christ Jesus were baptized into his death? Therefore we have been buried with him through baptism into death, in order that just as Christ was raised from the dead through the glory of the Father, so we too may live a new life" (Rom. 6:3–4 NET).

Put another way: we were planted with Christ and just as he sprung up in new life, so did we, baby.

When I came to this planting season, one of the things I personally wanted to let grow wild on my land was expansiveness. The teachers at my kids' school call this a growth mindset, and basically it means you don't see things like failure as anything but a challenge. Obstacles are invitations, not necessarily to success in this case, but to connection. I knew I wanted a plot of land that honored the curiosity I saw reflected in the Gospels, that left room for me to be wrong and for my wrongness not to threaten who God is, that was comfortable with me saying, "I don't really know."

One of the systems that died in my fire was the strict binary mentality that if A is true, B must be false; that if A is good, B must be bad. There are males, and there are females. You always do something, or you never do something. And it's not that a binary mentality is evil or wrong; it's just an overly simplified way of trying to figure out intricate problems.

This worked great for me at the beginning of my faith life, and I'm glad I had it. A faith outlook nestled in the binary helped me to better understand complex concepts: drunkenness is bad, and not drinking at all is good. Having sex before marriage is bad, not having sex is good. You get the idea. Perfectly acceptable ways for a baby with a cake-batter brain to look at the world.

But as you now know, that could not withstand my intentional arson.

And this can be terrifying because that binary thinking is a very safe place. But a growth mindset around your faith feels more like what I imagine happens when a roller coaster pulls off the platform and you realize you're not strapped in properly.

Once you've burned away the binary, once you begin engaging beyond A and B, you see the truth about the cognitive dissonance between what you understood to be true and what is actually true (there it is: the truth again). And now you have to be free.

And no matter how you've gone through this process, what I hope more than anything in this whole world is that you've gotten free. I don't know what freedom looks like or which choices you made about replanting. But here are some of the options I see available to you as you grapple with what your freedom could offer.

One path is to decide what you struggled with wasn't really all that big of a deal. That is to say, you essentially land back where you started, relatively unchanged after your journey (drink). I don't think this disentanglement experience has to mean you're suddenly ready to start protesting outside of every VBS. But it's entirely possible that, after you've done the work, you've found the original answers to be satisfactory. Whatever your pressure point was, you dealt with it. The good news is you did the work and you have a renewed confidence in your faith journey (drink!). Nothing bad about that.

Another path could be you now find yourself completely and totally at odds with the institution of Christianity, so much so that you are persuaded to step away from organized Christianity or deconvert altogether. I absolutely see why someone would choose (or even feel morally compelled) to walk this path. I've flirted with it and ultimately it's not for me, but to uproot a belief system you've held your entire life and walk away to the sounds of everyone in your life (probably) freaking out? I think that takes a lot of courage.

Whatever it is you're looking for, I sincerely hope you find it. I mean that. I've also found former Christians to be the most clear-eyed critics of our faith; they tend to hear with extreme clarity the things we register as background noise. As painful as it can be to hear it, their critiques of our faith, if they are willing to share, are a gift—one we are wise to learn from.

But maybe you deconstructed and reconstructed yourself into a new place that still feels familiar: the way you hold your beliefs is different, and some things have changed, but you would still check that "Christian" box on a survey if you were pressed. This was (and still kind of is) me: one foot out, railing against the injustices perpetuated by the church and one foot in, blasting a Hillsong album and cathartically bawling outside a Taco Bell, Mexican pizza cheese dripping off my steering wheel.

I can't speak to the experience of landing in a place of "here I am again, back where I began" or deconversion, although I see you. But if you are with me in the Taco Bell parking lot, let's talk it out.

I mean, go get your Crunchwrap Supreme first, and then we'll talk out what it means when you leave the realm of binary thinking and find yourself Conflictedly Christian.

Being Conflictedly Christian feels shameful sometimes. In fact, let's do a quick check on all the ways this made me feel, and you can raise your hand when I call out something you resonate with:

Ashamed
Inauthentic
Isolated
Annoyed
Helpless

Inadequate

Anxious

Angry

Adrift

If you resonated with any of these feelings, you might qualify for placement in our Conflictedly Christian Program. I felt as if I didn't take the suffering perpetuated by the church onto other people seriously enough. I wasn't willing to call out systemic issues within a structured institution because it benefited me in some way, making me a fair-weather ally to my friends and family who agonized under the burden of the truly awful abuses committed in the name and for the advancement of power in Christianity.

Are you allowed to exist within a system and also call for it to be held accountable? Is it possible to make changes from inside an institution, or is that something people who are afraid to leave say? Am I a coward if I benefit from the community aspect of Christianity and all its trappings when I know others do not have the luxury of that community because they support fill-in-the-blank or they are fill-in-the-blank? Is what's best for me also best for my family? What does it mean to apply the label of Christian to me at all? Can I love the ceremony and ritual of Christianity, even if I have to dig and sift to find the pre-empire version of it? Is all of this (*gestures wildly, takes a long pull on a fake cigarette*) just an exercise in me justifying my own faith to myself, when really I am simply a cog in the Giant American Religious Complex, a meal for the machine, Soylent Green for God and Country, wasting my one precious life following rules that don't matter for a god that doesn't exist but I've been programmed to think does AND loves me for the benefit of a compliant society?

Is it morally good to be a Christian? Is it all-or-nothing? Do I have to choose between toxic, abusive Christianity, or no Christianity at all?

These are questions we have to wrestle with (oh, gah, she wants us to wrestle again). And if we are committed to honoring our baptism of hope while telling the truth, we need to look all that fear in the face.

The list of ways Christianity has been misused and abused is long and can look really different depending on who you're talking to. Some people might think affirming churches walking in a Pride parade is heresy; some people might think holding a MAGA rally in your sanctuary is heresy. The point is, when we say, "The name of Jesus has been misused and abused," there's a 50-ish percent chance we don't even agree on what that means. But I don't think it does us any good to pretend we don't see it.

So how are we supposed to make sense of this behemoth of Christianity, with all its baggage and all its easy-yokeness, that can be so good and so terrible, depending on who's talking and who's asking? Like I said, it's no wonder we all feel like we can't see straight.

And it's beyond difficult to bust out of this kind of thinking because of the way it's so deeply ingrained in our brains. It's almost like going from 3D to 4D but trying to explain 4D to someone who has never experienced 4D. Except the person who has never experienced 4D is yourself. But we're no strangers to doing much more difficult things at this point, so I believe in us. We can move along a spectrum instead of living in a binary this or that, an all or nothing kind of existence.

Binary code is how we tell computers what to do, which I guess is a thing that happens for a certain subset of people with bigger brains. I like this definition from a website called

"The Kids Should See This," which means it's for children, and because I am a theater person and not a computer person, I can follow it: "Imagine trying to use words to describe every scene in a film, every note in a song, or every street in your town. Now imagine trying to do it using only the numbers 1 and 0. Every time you use the Internet to watch a movie, listen to music, or check directions, that's exactly what your device is doing, using the language of binary code."[1]

Within the combination of zeros and ones lies the EN-TIRETY OF THE INTERNET. These people aren't even pulling the twos in, and they are doing all of the internet. Everything from our archived Tumblr posts to Taylor Swift Eras Tour tickets to messages from your best friend who lives halfway across the globe. The whole World Wide Web is contained within the binary code. The thing that made the credits for *The Matrix* is the sum total of our online lives: the good, the bad, the wonderful, the terrible—it's all there in ones and zeros.

I think the same is true for Christianity, for faith, for whatever you want to call what we're figuring out here. Within the zeros and ones, the good and the bad, there lies the entirety of the Christian religious experience. And that experience can fall all across the spectrum. Yes, the toxicity of Christianity is alive and well, just like it has been for over two thousand years. We're barely into the book of Acts before people start cooking the church books for their own gain. And these destructive powers (actually, calling them destructive powers takes away the accountability aspect: these are power-hungry people who have forgotten what their identities are found in) are having their way with the American church right now. Sexual abuse scandals in pretty much every denomination, perversions of power, leaders misusing Scripture to control their own private kingdoms, and the unholy union of Christian nationalism and white supremacy all rotate through the news cycle with almost perfect regularity. And they should. Bring it all out. Drag what is hidden into a million-watt spotlight. It's important that we talk about these things because they are not of God. It's crucial as believers and members of the institution that we give these no quarter in the house of the Lord. The only way the word *Christian* and the church universal will begin to regain any kind of witness in the world is if we start acting like people who love like and are loved by Jesus. People who aren't afraid of the truth.

Now this is on us. Now we have work to join.

So there's the bad, and we all know the bad. But there's also a lot of good. For all the mala fides, the bona fides remain. The zeros and ones contain it all, right? The good stuff doesn't make it onto the news because it's usually smaller and quieter, and that's okay. A pastor faithfully shepherds her flock for forty years. A small group stocks a local public school's emergency period supplies cabinet. A Sunday school class sets up a prayer calendar to carry one of their own as he receives cancer treatment. A youth group mobilizes to help a refugee family get settled in their new apartment. And of course, it's not just about the stuff we do. It's about the God we encounter, the Jesus we find, the Holy Spirit we meet, and the beloveds we are.

But, Erin, you say.

Erin, it feels like this country and even the world is so divided right now, and everyone can simply choose to interpret the Scriptures to suit their own proclivities or tax brackets. Some people say it's loving to cut a gay son out of their family, and some say it's loving to fully affirm and accept him for who he is. How can one person say Holy Spirit has led them to one conclusion and another person say Holy Spirit has led them to the opposite conclusion?

There must be a way to figure out how to separate the toxic version from the good stuff. There must be a standard we hold all this behavior, all these actions, all these belief systems to, something that helps us understand whether, under the light of Jesus, something will be illuminated or burned to a crisp. How do we know?

What will grow on our plot of land now? What ecosystems will be sustained? We may still have complicated feelings about Scripture, but that doesn't mean it doesn't have things to ponder here. Let's look at what might flourish now that the soil is ready to receive healthy plants.

First, we set the scene. In his letter to the Galatians, Paul is pissed at this church. The first part of this letter is basically Paul going off on them for forgetting who they are in Christ. When we get to chapter five, he's worked up a sweat. He wants to remind the church at Galatia what happens when someone uses the freedom God gave them for their own gain.

I played tennis in high school, and while it's not known for being much of a contact sport if you play it correctly, my dad was always my hype guy before I walked on the court. A series of high fives, various intense vocalizations, and a good amount of headbutting was involved, along with some version of the phrase "You wanna get fired up?" yelled entirely too loud for a tennis environment. When you read Galatians 5, that's what you should picture: me and my dad hyping you up, headbutting you, and yelling "You wanna get fired up?" over your shoulder.

The Message* puts it so colorfully. This is the fruit that grows on our land when it's sown with bad crops:

> Repetitive, loveless, cheap sex; a stinking accumulation of mental and emotional garbage; frenzied and joyless grabs for happiness; trinket gods; magic-show religion; paranoid loneliness; cutthroat competition; all-consuming-yet-never-satisfied wants; a brutal temper; an impotence to love or be loved; divided homes and divided lives; small-minded and lopsided pursuits; the vicious habit of depersonalizing everyone into a rival; uncontrolled and uncontrollable addictions; ugly parodies of community. I could go on. (Gal. 5:19–21)

This list is so specifically brutal because we all know exactly the ways we've traded the good love of God for false freedom and ended up on one of these dead-end streets. And this isn't God punishing us; we do that just fine on our own.

We promised ourselves back in an earlier chapter that hope is not real hope unless it comes honestly. And the honest truth is that sometimes it's easy to blame our spiritual malcontent on outside forces and not look inward. There is no question we often see some who claim the banner of God's own people perpetuating these exact things, maybe because they themselves are hurt, or they desire power, or any other of a multitude of reasons. But it's also true that we are not perfect. If we are strong enough to survive all the things perpetuated against us directly or indirectly, in the name of Jesus we are strong enough and loved by Jesus

---

*Here's another reason I love the Message: some of us have read these verses from Galatians a million times to the point they've become background noise: completely meaningless. The Message shakes up the language and reengages us, calling us back to attention.

enough to be honest about the ways we played (and will play) a part as well.

We can be sure if we recognize ourselves among Paul's list of ways to waste our freedom, something needs to be recalibrated. If any understanding of Scripture leads us to Paul's catalog of bad fruit, we need to rethink our interpretation. And if any action we do in the name of God leads us to these places, there's a fairly good chance we heard our own voice over God's.

But Paul says, like a drama queen, "I could go on." So, it's not as if this list is the be-all, end-all. How can we find a way to know if our interpretation or deed or relationship or thought is aligned with how God wants us to live when so many iterations of our faith vie for our attention? Let's keep going with Paul and see if he tells us.

"But what happens when we live God's way? He brings gifts into our lives, much the same way that fruit appears in an orchard—things like affection for others, exuberance about life, serenity. We develop a willingness to stick with things, a sense of compassion in the heart, and a conviction that a basic holiness permeates things and people. We find ourselves involved in loyal commitments, not needing to force our way in life, able to marshal and direct our energies wisely" (Gal. 5:22–23).

If you or a loved one has ever been traumatized by a Christian summer camp or VBS, you may be entitled to compensation, but you also might remember singing an unhinged song about the fruits of the Spirit. You say what the fruit of the Spirit is not (i.e., a watermelon or a strawberry) and then you list off the actual fruits of the Spirit: love, joy, peace, patience, kindness, goodness, faithfulness, gentleness, and self-control (oh-ol-sing it with me now).

Does this action or behavior or belief or interpretation align with these fruits? Then I know I'm at least headed in the right direction. I can, with genuineness of heart and honesty of mind, feel as confident as possible these are the places the God of the universe who loves me wants me to focus my spirit.

I want to be careful not to make this a checklist of behaviors that will make us right with God. We can't trade one version of legalism for another. These are not behaviors that "save" us or take the place of any kind of a relationship with Jesus. They are what overflows out of our lives when we are connected to God. They are what springs out of us when we are consistently anchored to God. Any of this motivated by guilt or shame is not of God; I really believe that.

What makes me beloved is that I am loved by God. When I show that to the world, when I embody that love, when I believe that, it looks like the fruits of the Spirit, but not because God sees us performing and silently approves of us. It looks like the fruits of the Spirit because that is what love does. When you are loved you are safe to return it with an outpouring of all these beautiful gifts.

Not all the time. Or let me speak for myself: I do not do this all the time. I judge harshly. I criticize based on actions rather than intentions. I react regrettably. I ruin friendships with my holier-than-thou attitude and elitist behaviors. I lay beloved souls on the altar of being right and bring my knife down. I still try to plant bad crops so often, so publicly, with such dramatic flair. I take a lot of comfort in Fr. Richard Rohr's words: "We grow spiritually much more by doing it wrong than by doing it right."[2]

At least I hope that is true. If it is, I feel like I should be further along now. Alas.

Within these ones and zeros is a paradigm for human flourishing. It has been bastardized. It has been commodified. Nationalized. Poorly represented. Hijacked. Lost its way. But with all my heart, I believe God has placed within us the thesis that every human is innately beloved, and when we love God, it leads, every time, to loving them. Not to belittling them. Not to demanding they conform to me. It would be so much easier if Jesus would, like Anne Lamott says, "command us to obsess over everything, to try to control and manipulate people, to try not to breathe at all, or to pay attention, stomp away to brood when people annoy us, and then eat a big bag of Hershey's Kisses in bed."[3]

I realize it's a little ridiculous to think a historical figure from the first century loves you. I realize it's objectively ludicrous to claim you love a first-century historical figure. Truly, if someone thought this way about Napoleon or Helen of Troy, you would work to get them help. It might be Stockholm syndrome. It might be an overactive imagination. Maybe I've been pickled in evangelical brine for too long. But I operate under the potentially delusional thinking that something divine worked in Paul's pen when he scrawled that he was "absolutely convinced" nothing, not one thing he could possibly imagine, not politics, not the past, not the future, not our successes, not our failures, not the things we question, not the things we let slide, not our half-baked theologies, not our problematic interpretations, not our poor attempts at love, not our hidden hatreds, not our wounds, not our bravery could separate us from God. If God is who God says they are, then it's really true that not one thing can keep us from God's love. Then the Good News that everyone talks about is really, actually true. And good. For everyone. I mean everyone. God truly loves us, and when we truly love God, when we live fully into our belovedness, and from that comes an outpouring that offers belovedness to others, the kingdom of God is at hand. And it is so beautiful.

We imperfect creatures are stumbling and grasping in the dark. Paul says one day we'll see clearly, and maybe he's right. Maybe he knows something we don't. But out of all the stories we've shot into the cosmos, for me one rings out clearer and sweeter than the others. One that asks impossible things of me while giving impossible gifts. One that does not promise answers but promises presence. One I see repeating all over the galaxy: death is never the final word, it's only the indicator of resurrection, the last word of the first chapter. On my good days, I believe this. On my hard days, I ask someone to believe for me. On my unfathomable days, God and I have it out. I throw the questions, I hurl the doubts, I fire the skepticism. I refuse to let go, and I notice I'm also being held. And when we've offered each other an uneasy truce, when I give the trappings of religion the side-eye and strike my match, I'm not alone.

Because Jesus is who he says he is, he stands with me as we watch it burn.

Because, every time, what remains is love.

I don't know where you'll end up when you close this book in a moment. I think if anything, I hope you know God is not threatened by your doubts, and you can have your questions. I hope you aren't afraid of wrestling like Jacob. I hope you loosen your grip on the need to be right. I hope you explore the outskirts of where you thought God lived. Most of all, I hope you lean into your belovedness—because for all the laments, questions, and pressure points, that is where good things will always grow.

AFTERWORD

Where Do We Go from Here?

The hardest thing on earth is choosing what matters.
Sue Monk Kidd, *The Secret Life of Bees*

Working out your faith is difficult. It can bring up a lot of heavy baggage and painful memories. It's not really a fun time. And even when you feel like maybe you can breathe a little inwardly, there are always other people bumping up against you. I'm sorry that life is going to get complicated outside the pages of this book. I'm sorry your partner or your parents or your people might not fully understand the places you've been, the ways you've changed, or the new growth cultivated on your little plot of land. Transformations are hard, internally and externally, and even when we know in our bones it's for good, not everyone will share that sentiment.

While I was writing this book, I started reading another book (do not recommend) that is pretty against the concept of deconstruction. The authors kind of (oh my gosh, it is so hard to give them the benefit of the doubt right now, but please know I am really trying) do their best not to villainize those who are "asking genuine questions" or have "suffered abuse," but the first line in the book is "apostasy is nothing new."[1] So you could say it sets a tone.

If you've been honest about your struggles with friends and family members who are maybe not comfortable with that honesty, you might be familiar with that tone. There are accusations, condescension, and anger when shared experiences don't align. We are quick to demonize, to cover our bases, to remind others we are not individually complicit in the sins and shortcomings of a greater community.

Another reason this gets tricky is because we've individualized faith so much that we think our freedom, spiritual or otherwise, doesn't impact anyone else's. This is why there is barely any cognitive dissonance for Christians in the United States celebrating Christmas while the birthplace of Jesus is bombed to hell and back. We just keep on with our Christmas teas and our Elf on the Shelf, because we are so disconnected from the fact that we belong to each other.

But we do belong to each other. We're going to share neighborhoods and schools and church pews and office buildings and dinner tables and beds with people who do not see things the way we see them. We're going to be in close proximity to people who will not be as committed to seeing our belovedness as we are committed to seeing theirs, which will, in turn, cause us to forget our commitment. Not everyone will be as comfortable with the idea of being wrong, not everyone will be able to tell the honest truth baptized in hope.

We're to rub elbows with people who think we're heretics. So how are we going to do that?

We have to love them anyway.

I've tried hard to stay away from requirements while writing this book because "have-tos" and "musts" aren't my deal. Plus, the Bible is clear on like five things, and I'm not sure I feel comfortable throwing around imperatives like candy. However, one of those things it is fairly clear on is the greatest commandment.

I don't get to be in charge of anyone else's life. I don't get to tell people how they can think or feel or act. I can disagree with it, I can actually hate it, but it is a flat-out obligation to see God in everyone. I say this to us all, but mainly to myself: if I'm leveling a claim of apostasy, if I'm making a statement that draws clear lines about who gets to sit at the banquet table of God and who doesn't, I better be damn sure I know what I'm talking about.

What was the point of this whole journey (drink) if it didn't move us in a more loving direction? Why did we even bother if what we sow is more of the same tired in-fighting and petty bickering?

The most radical thing you will do is really, truly love your neighbor, because the most radical thing someone else is doing is really, truly loving you. Our belovedness is tied to everyone else's. We cannot escape each other. This kind of love isn't pandering or easily manipulated; it says the difficult thing, it speaks the truth, but it never stops loving. It takes its work as a joy revolutionary seriously. It knows things are dire out there, so nothing will stop it from loving the hell out of everyone in the world. It's out here in the wild, in the desert, baptizing the truth with oceans of hope.

You just might be surprised who needs to know their own belovedness. And you just might be the person to help them see. You just might be the person who knows where to find a can of gasoline and a match.

ACKNOWLEDGMENTS

First, I want to thank Uncrustables; the Chick-fil-A drive-thrus at Hoover Commons (my girl Jamie is the best), Patton Creek (Wesley is a real one), and the Grove; DoorDash (although for the love, please stop using Google Maps); the Holiday Inn on John Hawkins Drive; and Airbnbs in Chattanooga and Cullman for providing non-human emotional support during the writing process.

My beloved Jonathan Merritt, who frequently took my phone calls while he was in the shower, patiently listening to me have a nervous breakdown. It takes an enormous amount of skill as an agent to manage someone's panic attack while also giving yourself a shampoo, but of course he is up to the task. Tenacious and no BS, he is, I am convinced, the finest agent known to humankind, and I am grateful for his friendship.

The entire team at Baker Publishing, specifically Brianna DeWitt. The fine people at Baker defied every preconceived notion and exceeded every expectation. I adore them all, and Brianna led the charge with so much love I felt like she cared about this book as much as I did. And I can't tell you what that means to an author. Brianna must be protected at all costs. Brian Vos is a total prince, and Lauren Cole saved me from so many copyediting errors I owe her an Edible Arrangement every day for the rest of my life.

A huge thanks to Jenna DeWitt and Dr. Jen Rosen for their sensitivity reads. Their generosity and insight helped me consider perspectives I don't naturally see, and they made this book better without question.

This book simply would not have existed without the benevolent interference of Stephanie Duncan Smith, who invited me up to Baker's headquarters to chat a few years before I even had an idea. At every single editing round, she challenged me, sharpened me, refused to let me take the easy way out, and hounded me to be better. I was a fine writer before, but she made this book into something it could never have been without her. Her excellence is inescapable between these covers.

A fine group of humans risked their reputations and good names to say nice things about this book, and in this day, that's a big deal. I'm really honored to have the kind and thoughtful endorsements of Pete Enns, Meredith Miller, Zach W. Lambert, Emily P. Freeman, Kendra Adachi, and I'm including Kat Armas in here, even though a sweet baby thwarted endorsement plans, as babies are wont to do.

I once sat on an airport floor (gross) during a very long layover, downloaded *Jesus Feminist* to my Kindle, and read the entire thing in one sitting (not gross). It rearranged my brain, and I became a Sarah Bessey acolyte right there between the Hudson News and the Chili's To-Go. I can't quite wrap my head around the fact she agreed to write a foreword for this book. Sarah has been a spiritual mother to me, and I am so grateful I get to share a timeline with her.

I am enormously grateful to my coworkers and colleagues at the PMG, especially Knox, Jamie, Jason, and Evan, for allowing me to have three (3) nervous breakdowns during work hours while writing this book, and for the ways they supported my endeavors through their kindness and marketing efforts. I know I work in a very special place with talented, generous, and kind people, and after working in some very special places of another sort, I am thankful to them.

Brother Jim and Patsy Hancock, Dan Tracy, David and Robin Lowery, John and Janet Butterfield, Mark and Cindy Stewart, Buddy and Cindy Townsend, Andy and Gwen Hicks, Misty Chitwood, Gary and Judy Kelley, Michael and Jana Kelley, Fr. Lyle and Mary Dorset, Hannah and Drew Francis, Chris Kinsley, Bronson and Leah Stewart, Hunter and Hannah Gregg, Ryan Kirkland, Nic and Rachel Seaborn, Hiram and Lene Rollo, Whitney Battle, Ish and Amber Pruitt, Amelia Breeze, Rita and Fred Lakeman, and Julie Buford. (I *know* there are others I am leaving out—please forgive me.) I have either been pastored by, watched you pastor, been taught by, or watched you teach, and it was/is a blessing in my life. You have good gifts, you so tenderly look after the people in your care, and you take your commission of love seriously. I have seen when no one else was looking, and your character is unmatched. Reader, if you ever have doubts that people in church leadership can be trustworthy, this list of names proves otherwise.

I have a small online community of genuinely some of the loveliest people on the internet. The Lil Swipes really don't know how they've buoyed me over the years, and their kindness means the world. I have a Post-it note on my computer from when I told them I was writing a book with a quote from a Lil Swipe, Carrie, who said, "Do the book. We will buy the book. Rave about the book. Become the book. LFG." That note did a lot of work for me during this process, and it reminded me that they care. I really do love y'all! And a special thanks to the dis/entangle beta group, which is how this whole thing got started. I loved sharing that space with y'all.

The Buford/Breeze/Lakeman Connect Group is my happy place. I didn't think I could ever be comfortable in a Sunday school class again, but Dip Night convinced me otherwise. Y'all are the best of the best and I love untangling faith with every single one of you.

A couple of times a week, I wake up at the un-Christlike time of 4:40 a.m. to work out with a group of women (and Nic). I really hate working out, but this practice has done more for my mental health, especially while writing, than I can possibly say. I desperately wish eating a brownie and drinking a glass of wine gave me the same emotional bene-fits as this practice does, but alas. These ladies probably have no clue how important the time I spend with them is to me, but I am really grateful for the daily butt-kickings we receive from Abigail Marie. While we're here, Molly Allen deserves thanks for being the best cheerleader a writer could ask for. In about twenty years, look for Molly's book on the *New York Times* bestseller list. Remember me when you're president, Molly!

To the ladies of the Magic Good Time group chat: There's no one I would rather cannonball into a pool with while singing "The Star-Spangled Banner." Thank you for being willing to carry the trouble, even though we had to rename the chat.

Megan Beam and Lauren Jennings are the smartest and most infinite people I know, and pizza nights in the Anda-lusia parlor are some of the most exquisite nights available on this planet.

If it's at all possible, please get yourself some cheerleaders like Retha Nichole, Courtney Cleveland, and Tara Bremer. Please find friends who will be honest with you about when they hate a book cover and will never come to a facts fight with feelings when it's about business (Courtney does come to a facts fight with feelings about all other things, however, but we wouldn't have it any other way). Please surround yourself with people who are not afraid to tell you when you're being stupid, when you're making mistakes, when your focus is off, when you're missing the plot. And if you can, make sure they love you deeply. That will make all the difference.

I would not get a daggone thing accomplished if it weren't for Hannah Gregg. She keeps me on task, she forces me to respond to emails, and she organizes me in a way that is loving but also says, please get your s-word together. The fact that she puts up with me at all is a gift, and having her in my life in any capacity is a gift. Also I will thank Ollie here for being the cutest baby born in the 2020s. His cuteness is inspirational to me.

Kendra Adachi has been a deeply generous friend to me in the realm of writing and publishing, and sometimes I pretend she is the big sister I never had. I have benefited from her wisdom and kindness and her Change Your Life Chicken, all of equal importance in my life.

It is because of a conversation with Sophie Hudson on a plane coming back from Chicago seven years ago that this book made it. It is because she was kind to a flailing, unsure ding-a-ling who needed some encouragement, but didn't even know that's what she needed. I would also like to thank Sophie and our friend Melanie Shankle for letting me tag along on their writer's retreat where I learned what writers do: watch college baseball, eat food, and stare at walls making unsavory grunting noises.

I don't know how it happened, but I fell into the safest bevy of women I've ever known. Amelia, Julie, Zana, Tris, Taylor, EN, and April: when can we go back to Star? Being a part of the Casserole Circle makes me feel like no matter how bad things get, everything is totally gonna be alright.

Women are amazing, and I've been loved by some of the greats: Morgan, Annie, Liza, Sass, Hannah, Ber, Tiffany, Brandi, Amanda, Cara, Malinda, Tristi, Jen, and Nemus. You loved me when I was inexplicably licking frogs in Mr. Tversky's biology class. You loved me when I punched Scott N. in the face on the tennis bus. You loved me when I took my shoes off in the student life van. You loved me when I ordered the wrong size of bridesmaid dress for your wedding. You loved me before I knew what self-awareness was. Thank you for not sharing my terrible eighth-grade poetry. Thank you for letting me live with you and your husband (and Bob Hedge!) in a two-bedroom apartment while we did the South Beach Diet. Thank you for folding me into your life when you married my friend and letting me be your friend too. Thank you for letting me insert myself in your life when we went to the UK. I love you all so much. You're so freaking special to me.

My heart is 50 percent blood, 50 percent pasta dishes eaten around a table with three other women who make up a group chat called The Subcommittee. Their friendship is the greatest gift of my forties, and they have found worlds in me I didn't know existed. Have you ever had a text thread kind of save you? It's like that.

Being an adult means you can make stuff up, so I pretend Katie Dickerson is my real sister, even though technically she's my sister-in-law. Thank you for teaching me about eyebrows and my nervous system and a good red lip. Your presence is warm and safe, and you are everyone's favorite person. But I am so lucky to call you my best friend.

One of the first women I ever saw teaching Sunday school was my grandmother, my Nene. She is the vanguard in the great contingent of people who taught me who Jesus is and how much he loves us. No one has taught me more about the fruits of the Spirit than my sweet Nene, and I am forever grateful to have had her example for my whole life.

I grew up in a home saturated in love and mutual respect, something I did not realize until much later was a rare gift. An older sister needs a little brother to keep her humble, and my little brother was up to the challenge. Drew has grown into a man of unwavering integrity, of firm conviction, of thoughtfulness, and he is such a credit to the line of men who bear his name. I am really honored to be his big sister, even though he once stole a bag of quarters from me and still claims I stole it from him. A lot of people have been shepherded by my father (he's taught Sunday school for over forty years), but only two of us can claim to be parented by him, which is a badge of honor I will wear proudly until the day I die. We don't agree on everything theologically, but my dad would never in a million lifetimes let a silly thing like that get in the way of loving anyone, especially me. My dad has believed in me my whole life: he has loved me into being a writer. You cannot imagine the kind of reckless self-confidence that gives a person. Now that I am a mother, I have a small inkling of what my mother gave to ensure I became a functioning member of society (she had an uphill battle at times), and it cannot be measured. My mom is the glory of our family: she gives not out of obligation or duty, but because she really loves Jesus and that love overflows onto literally every person she comes into contact with. You've never seen anything more beautiful than my mother loving someone, and I cannot tell you what a gift it is to be her daughter and to receive that love from the deepest part of her on a daily basis. If you ripped me open and cut out my heart, you'd read the names of these three humans all over it. They know the very worst of me and love me still. I love them with everything I have.

To my kids: What I hope is that when you eventually read this book, you won't hear anything different than what we've always talked about at the kitchen island, in the car driving to practice, or around chips and salsa at Frontera. I want you to find your identity in your belovedness. I want you to know you are deeply treasured by God and nothing can separate you from them.

Holland, my Hollsie-Wolls! Your tenderness challenges me to see Christ in everyone, even those who are hard to love. Your faith encourages me (not to mention so many others), and I love your inquisitive mind that is not afraid of spiritual questions. I am in awe of who you are becoming every day, and I am so proud to be your mom. It is a gift I will never get over. Whether we're having a deep theological conversation or watching *Dance Moms* on the couch, I am just delighted by you.

Marlo, my Bebe! You remind me that joy is medicine we all need, no matter how serious or hard things get. I know Jesus belly laughs with us on the regular because I just don't think anyone is as hilarious as you. God made you so special, with such unique gifts, and God is already blessing people with your friendship, your kindness, your fearlessness, and your dance moves. I wish everyone could see you break it down during our kitchen dance parties.

Cyrus, my Buddy! You ran into my heart so fast, just like Sonic, and I was never the same. What I love about you is whether we're watching Mob Battles (still not totally sure what they are), playing *Pokémon*, or going on a Mommy-Cyrus date, you go all in. You are excited about everything, and you give it 100 percent. The best snuggler, you take such good care of Chasey, and you are a sweet friend who knows how to keep it real. God gave you the gift of loving big, and it makes me so happy to be someone you love.

To my Ben: When I think about the process of working out what is contained in this book: kitchen talks and frustrated puzzle conversations and long car chats and tears and laughing and fights and all of it, what I keep coming back to is: I'm so glad it was you, I'm so glad it is you, and I am so glad it will be you. Thank you for waiting for me, for loving me back into myself, thank you for all the things too tender to put here. As our beloved Mr. Knightley says, "Perhaps it is our imperfections that make us so perfect for one another."[1]

NOTES

Introduction

1. Jeffrey M. Jones, "U.S. Church Membership Falls below Majority for First Time," Gallup.com, March 29, 2021, https://news.gallup.com /poll/341963/church-membership-falls-below-majority-first-time.aspx.

2. Pew Research Center, "In U.S., Decline of Christianity Continues at Rapid Pace," Pew Research Center's Religion & Public Life Project, October 17, 2019, https://www.pewresearch.org/religion/2019/10/17/in -u-s-decline-of-christianity-continues-at-rapid-pace/.

3. Michael Lipka, "Why America's 'Nones' Left Religion Behind," Pew Research Center, August 24, 2016, https://www.pewresearch.org/fact -tank/2016/08/24/why-americas-nones-left-religion-behind/.

4. Relevant Staff, "Deconstruction Doesn't Mean You're Losing Your Faith," *Relevant Magazine*, December 1, 2021, https://relevant magazine.com/magazine/how-to-deconstruct-your-faith-without-los ing-it/.

5. Aaron Earls, "Most Teenagers Drop Out of Church When They Become Young Adults," Lifeway Research, January 15, 2019, https:// research.lifeway.com/2019/01/15/most-teenagers-drop-out-of-church-as -young-adults/.

6. Kevin Singer and Josh Packard, "Trust in Religious Institutions Is Low among Gen Z—but Young People Are Keeping the Faith in Other Ways," *Religion in Public*, February 19, 2021, https://religioninpublic .blog/2021/02/19/trust-in-religious-institutions-is-low-among-gen-z-but -young-people-are-keeping-the-faith-in-other-ways/.

Like a Wrecking Ball

1. Julian of Norwich, *Revelations of Divine Love*, ed. Grace Harriet Warrack (London, UK: Methuen, 1901), 153.

2. Anne Lamott, *Bird by Bird: Some Instructions on Writing and Life* (New York: Anchor Books, 1995), 187.

3. Father Richard Rohr, "The Resurrection of All Things," Center for Action and Contemplation, April 10, 2023, https://cac.org/daily-meditations/the-resurrection-of-all-things-2023-04-10/.

White Lion Hot Dog Jonathan Jesus

1. Mary-Frances O'Connor, *The Grieving Brain: The Surprising Science of How We Learn from Love and Loss* (New York: HarperOne, 2023), 5.

2. James Baldwin, *Nobody Knows My Name* (New York: Vintage Books, 1993), 117.

3. John Green, *The Fault in Our Stars* (New York: Penguin Books, 2014), 286.

4. Kate Bowler, *Everything Happens for a Reason: And Other Lies I've Loved* (New York: Random House, 2018), 118.

A Baptist Sits Shiva

1. Anne Lamott, *Help, Thanks, Wow: The Three Essential Prayers* (New York: Riverhead Books, 2012), Kindle.

2. Amanda Held Opelt, *A Hole in the World: Finding Hope in Rituals of Grief and Healing* (New York: Worthy Books, 2022), 27.

3. Fred Rogers, *You Are Special: Neighborly Words of Wisdom from Mister Rogers* (New York: Penguin Books, 1995), 115.

4. Brennan Manning, *The Wisdom of Tenderness: What Happens When God's Fierce Mercy Transforms Our Lives* (New York: HarperOne, 2004), 48.

What If the Wrestling Is the Point?

1. Brian Kolodiejchuk, ed., *Mother Teresa: Come Be My Light: The Private Writings of the "Saint of Calcutta"* (New York: Image, 2007), 169.

2. Joshua DuBois, "On Faith: Martin Luther King Jr.'s Struggles Can Lead Way for Obama as He Faces Difficulties," *Washington Post*, January 19, 2014, https://www.washingtonpost.com/lifestyle/style/on-faith-martin-luther-king-jrs-struggles-can-lead-way-for-obama-as-he-faces-difficulties/2014/01/19/7d9a9b48-7f90-11e3-9556-4a4bf7bcbd84_story.html.

3. Eric W. Gritsch, "Martin Luther's Humor," *Word & World* 32, no. 2 (Spring 2012): 139, https://wordandworld.luthersem.edu/wp-content/up loads/pdfs/32-2_Humor/Martin%20Luther's%20Humor.pdf.

4. Henri J. M. Nouwen, *Life of the Beloved: Spiritual Living in a Secular World* (New York: Crossroad Publishing Company, 2002), 48.

5. Barbara Brown Taylor, *Learning to Walk in the Dark* (New York: HarperOne, 2015), 85.

Avoidance Tactics and Other Games Our Brains Play

1. Ralph Lewis, "What Actually Is a Belief? And Why Is It So Hard to Change?," *Psychology Today*, October 7, 2018, https://www.psycholo-gytoday.com/us/blog/finding-purpose/201810/what-actually-is-belief-and -why-is-it-so-hard-change.

2. Mary Grace Garis, "What Happens When a New Lived Reality Forces You to Change Your Mind, According to a Neurologist and Psychologist," Well+Good, June 12, 2020, https://www.wellandgood.com /changing-your-mind-set/.

3. K. C. Cole, "Brain's Use of Shortcuts Can Be a Route to Bias: Perception: The Mind Relies on Stereotypes to Make Fast Decisions. But in Hiring, That Can Lead to Discrimination," *Los Angeles Times*, May 1, 1995, https://www.latimes.com/archives/la-xpm-1995-05-01-mn-61017 -story.html.

4. Mariam Arain et al., "Maturation of the Adolescent Brain," *Neuropsychiatric Disease and Treatment* (April 2013): 449–61, https://doi .org/10.2147/ndt.s39776.

5. Alison Escalante, "Scientists Think They Just Found the Brain's Spirituality Network," *Forbes*, August 24, 2021, https://www.forbes.com/sites/ alisonescalante/2021/08/24/scientists-think-they-just-found-the-brains-spirituality-network/?sh=1123286319b4.

6. David Biello, "Searching for God in the Brain," *Scientific American*, October 1, 2007, https://www.scientificamerican.com/article/searching -for-god-in-the-brain/.

7. René J. Muller, "Neurotheology: Are We Hardwired for God?," *Psychiatric Times*, May 1, 2008, https://www.psychiatrictimes.com/view /neurotheology-are-we-hardwired-god.

8. Frank Meshberger, "An Interpretation of Michelangelo's *Creation of Adam* Based on Neuroanatomy," *JAMA* 264, no. 14 (1990): 1837–41.

9. Ian Suk and Rafael Tamargo, "Concealed Neuroanatomy in Michelangelo's *Separation of Light From Darkness* in the Sistine Chapel," *Neurosurgery* 66, no. 5 (May 2010): 851–61, https://doi.org/10.1227/01 .NEU.0000368101.34523.E1.

10. Michelangelo Buonarroti, "To the Supreme Being," PoemHunter .com, n.d., https://www.poemhunter.com/poem/to-the-supreme-being/.

What Makes Faith So Hard, and What Compels Me to Stay

1. Patricia C. Hodgell, *Seeker's Mask* (Wake Forest, NC: Baen Books, 2007), Kindle.

2. Brennan Manning, *The Ragamuffin Gospel: Good News for the Bedraggled, Beat-Up, and Burnt-Out* (Portland: Multnomah Books, 2015), 168.

Your Unsoothed Heart Is Your Most Powerful Weapon

1. *Iconoclasts*, season 2, episode 6, "Dave Chappelle & Maya Angelou," directed by Joe Berlinger, featuring Dave Chappelle and Maya Angelou, aired November 30, 2006, on Sundance Channel.

2. Louisa May Alcott, *Little Women* (New York: Macmillan Collector's Library, 2004), 110.

3. Alcott, *Little Women*, 110.

4. *Little Women*, directed by Greta Gerwig (Culver City, CA: Columbia Pictures, 2019), DVD.

5. Jude Dry, "Greta Gerwig on the Pivotal 'Little Women' Scene Laura Dern Helped Inspire," IndieWire, November 15, 2019, https://www.indie wire.com/features/general/greta-gerwig-laura-dern-little-women-inside-actors-studio-1202189692/.

Foraging in the Wilderness

1. Richard Rohr, *The Universal Christ: How a Forgotten Reality Can Change Everything We See, Hope For, and Believe* (New York: Convergent Books, 2019), 49.

2. Krista Tippett, *Becoming Wise: An Inquiry into the Mystery and Art of Living* (New York: Penguin Books, 2016), 187.

But What If You're Wrong?

1. Barbara Brown Taylor, *An Altar in the World: A Geography of Faith* (New York: HarperOne, 2010), 33.

2. C. G. Jung, *Modern Man in Search of a Soul* (Eastford, CT: Martino Fine Books, 2017), 271.

How Does Your Garden Grow?

1. José Américo N L F de Freitas, "How Exactly Does Binary Code Work?," The Kids Should See This, July 12, 2018, https://thekidsshould seethis.com/post/how-exactly-does-binary-code-work.

2. Richard Rohr, *Falling Upward, Revised and Updated: A Spirituality for the Two Halves of Life* (Hoboken, NJ: Jossey-Bass, 2023), Kindle.

3. Anne Lamott, *Plan B: Further Thoughts on Faith* (New York: Riverhead, 2006), 224.

Afterword

1. Alisa Childers and Tim Barnett, *The Deconstruction of Christianity: What It Is, Why It's Destructive, and How to Respond* (Carol Stream, IL: Tyndale Elevate, 2023), 1.

Acknowledgments

1. *Emma*, directed by Douglas McGrath (Miramax Films, 1996), DVD.

ERIN HICKS MOON is a writer, podcaster, and storyteller who helps people disentangle faith by creating a kind and curious community that welcomes honest doubt and questions. She is the Resident Bible Scholar and host of the *Faith Adjacent* podcast, and senior creative at Podcast Media Group. Her popular weekly newsletter, "The Swipe Up," has garnered nearly twenty thousand highly engaged subscribers, and she has written and produced several popular Bible study guides. She lives in Birmingham, Alabama, with her husband and three children.

Connect with Erin:

ErinHMoon.com

 @ErinHMoon

 @ErinHMoon